PARENTING PLUGGED-IN TEENS

PARENTING PLUGGED-IN TEENS

Becoming Their GPS
in a Cyber-Sexual World

Elizabeth L. Clark, LPC

LIGHTNING SOURCE EDITION

Elizabeth L. Clark
Grand Junction, CO 81501

Cartoon art on cover by Mike Smith
Book design by Shelly L. Francis

This book is not intended to dispense medical or professional advice or replace parental wisdom.

Publisher's Cataloging-in-Publication Data
Clark, Elizabeth L.
Parenting plugged-in teens: becoming their GPS in a cyber-sexual world
p. cm
ISBN 978-0-9836203-2-7
1. Teenagers - Sexual behavior. 2. Parenting. I. Title
HQ27.C 2012
649'65--dc21

Ebook ISBN 978-0-9836203-3-4

To the blackbird singing in the dead of night, Kat, for asking...

Many Thanks

Thanks to a crew of critics, editors, and cheerleaders who helped expedite this book. The names Ann, Vickie, Lori, Nancy, and Melinda come to mind as masterful influencers of improvement: Bridget, the restructurer who insists that both bologna and good books must stand on their own; Rod, my clean-up king; and Mary Beth, Jacqueline, and our Bliss-Bless blogging Emily, without their blessed cheering this book would never have crossed the finish line. Mike Smith is cartoonist and driver extraordinaire. My deepest love and gratitude goes to Shelly Louise, who takes my rumpled piles of words, insists that I iron, then pushes a few magic buttons and transforms them into a glorious book...a rather handy skill; and to Kevin, who continues to nod confidently at me.

Contents

Prologue

When my now twenty-something year-old daughter was early into her freshman year of high school, she did something remarkable that encouraged me to do something remarkable. I had given her the draft of a teen novel I'd just finished. If you are family member of a writer you know that writers always give things they've written to their family to read. You probably also know that you must say you love the piece. You must also prove you read it by giving three examples of things you loved from the many pages you skimmed.

Since I write for teens and children, my poor daughter was forced to spend many of the hours she would have preferred spending with Harry and Hermione reading my stories instead. But she enjoyed luxuries such as warm clothing, shampoo and food, so she diligently read what I handed her and smiled. (I didn't really withhold necessities, but the threat may have been inferred.)

She handed me back this particular manuscript and perfunctorily told me three things she liked about it. Satisfied by her hunger-induced enthusiasm, I concluded the book was indeed destined to make even J.K. envious. I told her she could have dinner.

As she left the room she said over her shoulder, "I'd like more on that." Then she went straight to the kitchen for a bowl of cold porridge, (or maybe something less Dickens-ish, like Honey Nut Cheerios.)

I looked at the manuscript in my hands and saw that one of the pages had a corner folded over. Curious to see which of my clever words had inspired her to dog-ear a page I quickly read the text.

Surprisingly, it was not a part I thought was Pulitzer-worthy. It was a little speech made by the sweet and kind main character, Joe, about sex.

"I'd like more on that."

Even though I'd been a therapist for teens for more than two decades I had never broached the topic of sexuality in my writing, because it can be dicey with parents and belief systems. Yet, I'd been inspired by conversations about sex I'd recently had with some teens. I noticed a shift occurring in the things they were telling me. Something was changing and not for the better.

Until that point it seemed teens were as curious and awkward and confused as we had been about sex when we were their age. They fumbled around in the back seats of cars as we had. Their parents were talking to them as little as our parents had talked to us about sex. But in the end, we and they figured it out, fairly slowly, mostly safely.

The same sorts of kids were at risk for early and high-risk sex as when we were kids. Not much had changed until the mid-2000s. I now know that was when the Internet began to take over the teaching and modeling of sex for teens. I did not know it at the time.

That was when teens began talking about sex differently. They were more confused and having many more bad sexual experiences. Girls were getting physically and emotionally injured, and boys were feeling significantly more pressured and guilty than ever before. It wasn't that more teens were having sex. It was the quality, having gone from awkward to almost abusive.

It is important to note that there were also amazingly positive changes going on with this group as a whole. Something spectacular was happening to their self-confidence, their non-sexual social skills, their communication, their sense of security and connection, and their ability to take in and integrate information quickly. Again, I did not know these were related to their being constantly plugged-in to the Internet, but I am fairly certain it was and is.

But the changing sexual climate overpowered and darkened these positives changes.

I'd taken a small and cautious stab at addressing all these issues in my manuscript. My daughter, the kid who would never, ever, ever talk with me about sex in the past was suddenly saying "I'd like more on that."

Huh.

We all have a few moments of brilliance when we choose the right path. This was my moment. I spent the next six months researching teen sexuality, looking at current cultural trends that might be affecting teen sexuality, talking to everyone I could about sexuality in general, exploring my own personal experiences and beliefs, and tapping into my twenty-plus years of counseling teens so that I could give my daughter more on that.

I wrote a seventy-five page manifesto on the wisdom I wanted her to have about sexuality. Then I gave it to her. She took it, went to her room and stayed there for hours. When she emerged she handed it back to me, looked me in the eyes and said, "Thank you so much."

Thank you so much. Really?

And she meant it. She didn't mention three things she liked about it. She didn't need to because she had just looked me in the eyes and said, "Thank you so much."

I don't know why I didn't just give her the book to keep, but I didn't. I took it back when she handed it to me. I gave it to her when she asked for it a few months later. I took it when she handed it to me again. I gave it to her and took it back from her at least a dozen times over the course of her high school years. She always said "Thank you," but even better, we began to have conversations about sexuality.

She ended up navigating her mind, soul and, more importantly, body through those teen years well. Looking back I am certain that book full of my wisdom altered the course of her life. Decisions were made differently than decisions would have been made without my wisdom. (I'm pretty sure some of those altered decisions now have many children and a few mug shots.)

As she sailed safely into her adulthood I came to the conclusion that I'd written the greatest book ever on teen sexuality. I began doing research to prove my greatness. Though I found that I had done some good work and blindly followed the best advice on influencing my teen's sexual choices, I also found disappointing statistics for me but great news for all other parents. I found that all parents who talk mindfully about sex to their kids have kids who go slower and safer into their sexual lives. I had simply added to that statistic.

I found that you don't have to write a book, but you do have to be mindful. (Though it is a great book!).

PART I:
USING CURRENT LOCATION

I hear her through my office door; not her words, just the anger in her tone as she responds to her mother's polite waiting-room voice.

Her secret cyber-life has been exposed. She's been exposed. She's been humiliated at school, home, and with her extended family. To add insult to injury she now has to talk to some therapist as if she is insane.

She has absolutely no control over her life right now; no phone, no cyber connection, no social connection, so she has decided not to talk to me. Silence is the one stand she can take. She thinks that even though her mother seems sweet and concerned waiting in this office, she's really just waiting to tell the therapist every recently discovered detail of her daughter's cyber-sexual world. She probably already has. She's partially right. This mom did tell me everything over the phone, but not in a thrilled manner. No, she told me through tears of confusion and fear.

Game face. I open the door.

I shake her mother's hand. I shake the girl's boneless hand. I do not invite the mother into my office.

Alone with the kid, I smile slightly.

"You okay?" I let her know I have been informed.

She shrugs.

"It'll get better."

She huffs, but she hears that I have casually inferred this happens a lot, that she isn't alone, that there might be an end to this shame and guilt and humiliation, that there might be a way back to the life that got away from her.

Her exiled words begin to flow.

Chapter 1:

Happiness is North

You must know the only thing parents want for their children is happiness. As Dickens once said, "This must be distinctly understood or nothing wonderful can come of the story I am going to relate."

They were sound sleepers, my parents. Like most parents, they believed it takes great effort to raise happy children. It wore them out daily.

"Mom? Dad?" I would mouth in the darkness of their room with no sound, not even a whisper.

From the time I could toddle I woke up in the night pondering things I could not understand. These concepts like cruelty, want, self-doubt, and of course, death came in waves. As I aged, they mixed with the sexual-awakening concepts of power, and pulsing and fury over constraints.

Like black shadows creeping across my walls, these tormentors insisted I make the journey out of innocence into, at best, wisdom, but without wise guides more likely I'd stumble into ignorance, terror, or worse, closed-eyed apathy.

Mom?

Dad?

I grew up in a time when walking into your parent's room in the middle of the night was a sign of weakness. If I woke them I was met with an angry, "What's wrong?"

How could I possibly voice what I did not understand?

Without fever or vomit or need of a drink came a gruff, "Go back to bed."

Why did I stand barefoot on their cold floor night after night mouthing their names? Because I wished and hoped every time that they would wake up and ask, "What do you need?" Then I would say honestly, "I don't know...maybe directions." They would scoot over and let me under their warm blankets. They would begin to whisper ways to get from here to there with smooth and sure voices, proving themselves to be the wise navigators I knew they were.

Then I could cross that bridge from innocence to wisdom gracefully. I would know the balance of dark and light. I would be deeply grateful for kindness, courage, beauty and celebration, and I would nod to the presence of cruelty, fear, ugliness and oppression.

I can only imagine both the balm and poison of the cyber-world that is the landscape of adolescents on dark, cold nights as they struggle to find ways to grow-up wise.

Just as we did when we were their age, they really want directions through their sexuality, because they are walking around in bodies that rev like Ferraris. The desire to take it for a ride is tremendous, but teens aren't so good at asking for directions. Behind an abundant use of the words Dude and like, they silently scream: *Mom? Dad? Someone?*

Parents have rarely talked directly and honestly with their teens about sex, yet we live in a time when we can no longer follow this precedent. This is because an odd and perfect storm began brewing over a decade ago when weary parents handed over most sex education to schools just as schools were mandated to only tell them to wait until marriage, just as the average age of marriage increased to twenty-seven, just as a twenty percent drop in marriages occurred, just as television and movies became extremely sexually explicit, just as we plugged them in with phones and laptops and music pods and gaming systems that welcomed them into Pinocchio's Pleasure Island of cyber-sex, sexting and the mother of all current teen sexual modeling, Internet porn.

We have to know deep down that this has had tremendous consequences on their sexuality, their relationships, and therefore on their current and future happiness.

Mom? Dad?

In navigation terms, happiness is north: the constant that aligns us at all times. The core of every goal we have for our kids really is happiness because happy people are more connected, more creative, successful problem solvers, intimate, skilled with something to give to their community, educated enough, wealthy enough, self-confident, and content. Sexually healthy people are more physically fit, better able to reduce and release stress, and happier than sexually unhealthy folks.

We can become the voice of their GPS and help them bridge the worlds between Pixar and cyber-sexuality. It is actually quite easy. This is because they are confused and disappointed with the sexual experiences they are having, and because they are also quite skilled at integrating true information and sharing it with their peers instantly. Happiness is really just a few right and left turns away.

Chapter 2:
Of Course They Are...

Of course they are...viewing porn, sexting and cyber-sexing, or they will be soon, or they will be affected by it. How old were they when we handed them the cell phone, lap top, gaming system, music pod?

We did so with the best of intentions; to keep them connected to us and others and safety. We did so to keep them technologically savvy in a world where that is a vital skill. We did so because these things were cool and fun and full of possibilities.

We distantly knew they might access darker sites, mostly sexual, but they were young and excited by exploring clever games and researching school projects. They showed no signs of being interested or affected by that sexual world. We hoped they would pass it by the same way we chose not to enter strip clubs and adult book stores.

We hoped.

Currently kids start watching porn around the age of eleven. Teen boys watch about twenty minutes of porn a day. About a third of teen girls have sent nude photos of themselves across the wireless waves. Young people under the age of twenty cannot distinguish the difference between porn-inspired sex and non-porn-inspired sex. The sex modeled in porn is anonymous, fast, disconnected, and degrading and physically harmful to women. Yet at the end of a porn sexual encounter everyone seems satisfied, having had a great time.

These aren't someone else's kids we're talking about. These are our kids. So, once again: *our* kids start watching porn around the age of eleven. *Our* teen boys watch about twenty minutes of porn a day. Over a third of *our* teen girls have sent nude photos of themselves across the wireless waves. *Our* young people under the age of twenty cannot distinguish the difference between porn inspired sex and non-porn inspired sex. The sex modeled in porn is anonymous, fast, disconnected, and degrading and physically harmful to women. Yet at the end of a porn sexual encounter everyone seems satisfied, having had a great time.

Unless your home is void of technology and you keep your children away from school and peers, then your kids are either participating in cyber-sexuality, or they will be soon, or their friends and romantic/sexual partners, present and future, will be.

Go back in time, Wayne's World-esque, to your teen years. Your body is alive with hormones, curiosity, and desire. What if you had technology that took you to private places chock-full of images that lit up your body, places where you could be completely anonymous and therefore sexual without obvious consequences? Would you ride that rollercoaster? Maybe? Probably?

So, what do we do? Ban porn? Good luck. I hope you are a professional lobbyist with tons of money. I am not. Should we parental-control all our kids' technology into sexual safety? Good luck with that, too. I hope you are a Wozniak, Gates, or Jobs techno-genius because every kid under the age of twenty is, and they are highly motivated to use their skills to keep all technology accessible to them.

As a therapist I live in the world of accepting what is, assessing the consequences of the situation, and addressing it with honesty, courage and wisdom. (It's not a great bumper sticker, but a good creed.)

Accepting that what is currently occurring is indeed currently occurring is the best path to healing. Screaming "this should not be" as the wave of a tsunami crests your coastal town wastes the energy you need to respond. "This should not be" are the four most often used words in moments of crisis, and they seldom help. The words that must take their place are "What do we do?"

Accept that cyber-sexuality which includes sexting, cyber-sex, and Internet porn, are here to stay and our children have almost unlimited access to it.

This should not be.

Wait, cancel that. What do we do?

Chapter 3:
Of Course We Are...Wise

Even more important than accepting our children's cyber-sexual reality, we must accept our own wisdom. We must accept that when we give a little wisdom to our children we have more influence over their sexual behaviors and choices than their peers, all media including porn, written material, and sex education. That is, when we give them a little wisdom.

But we don't. Not often.

We give them so much: braces, violin lessons, all the latest technology, haircuts, lunch money, vacations, and ferrets named Fred. We spend a lot of time fretting over their friends, piercings and tattoos, corn syrup, field time, college acceptance, prom dresses, ACT scores, the length of their shorts, and how far down their skinny hips their jeans fall.

We give them a great deal of our time and money and energy.

But our wisdom? Not so much. We're miserly with that, like folks who don't think they have two dimes to rub together. We simply don't know we have the wisdom they need. So currently it is their peers and the media that most influence teens' sexuality. Not us.

We could be the voice of their GPS and we're not speaking.

When did parents decide they weren't all that wise? When did our culture stop acknowledging the wisdom of age? When did we forget that our kids were not experienced or wise, but simply quite skilled at eye-rolling and programming our TVs and ring-tones?

What is this elusive wisdom we don't know we have? Parental wisdom is our truths based on a lifetime's worth of experiences, mindfully given with respect and honesty. (This definition was handed me by God himself, not on a stone tablet but in the shining eyes of well-parented teens.) Based on that definition, it is clear that we can all be wise parents.

We are wise. We've lived and seen the good, the bad, the ugly, and the beautiful in our living. We've tried to make sense of our choices and blessings and hardships. We were once young and our bodies were on fire like theirs are. We know how we handled it. We know what we would like for our kids. We do? Oh yes, all we want for our children is for them to be happy.

The braces and the fretting over colleges and ear gauges are all efforts to get them to happiness.

We really are it, the most influential people in our children's sexual lives. We have the Golden Ticket, we have the Genie's three wishes, we know the lotto numbers, we are the wise heroes in this movie.

And if we rip up that Golden Ticket, if we don't rub that lamp, if we don't play those lotto numbers, if we don't come in on cue then our understudy will go on for us, and that understudy is some teenager who has been given as little wisdom on sexuality as our kids have; therefore, they've gotten their wisdom from TV and movies; they've gotten their wisdom from Internet porn. They don't know the way.

But it is important to acknowledge something right now. I said this was going to be easy. I made it sound like we have all the answers. I lied. I did not acknowledge one particular issue: our culture is swimming in confusion about sexuality. Right? Think of your own sex life. About seventy-seven percent of adults are not in nuclear/monogamous families or, if so, it's the second, third, or fourth attempt. Teens aren't the only ones getting sexual on-line. A significant number of married adults are on Match-type romantic meeting sites. Many married folks report unsatisfactory sex lives. Where is that wisdom I say we are all so full of?

It is true that we don't have all the answers, but we really do have the basics that will help this crew of kids who have been awakened to sexuality not with the nudge of adolescence, but by a blaring alarm in the middle of childhood. We aren't going to answer all the issues around sexuality in our culture, but we can point our kids in the right direction, even if we aren't exactly there. We do know which way is north.

Of course we are wise...enough.

Chapter 4:
Of Course They Are...Thirsty

"I'm thirsty."

How many times as a parent have we heard and responded to this request? We hydrate our darlings like no other from breast to bottle, bottle to Sippy-cup, Sippy-cup to juice box, juice box to water bottles. We are always at the ready to quench parched mouths.

There are times when they are ill and don't ask for a drink, but we know of their need by their glassy eyes and fevered forehead. We hand them a cup of cool juice or honeyed tea and they take it with weak hands, drink with quivering lips and experience relief.

Our kids are not asking, but they are thirsty. I promise you.

Please believe me when I say they are thirsty because when you attempt to talk about the effects of the cyber world on their sexual lives they will probably roll their terrible eyes, huff with superiority and scream "I don't want to talk about this." You might believe they just downed the equivalent of gallon of Internet Wisdom Gatorade (a new flavor set to come out next year, I'm sure.) Don't be fooled.

Surveys of teens say they wish their parents would talk to them more about sex. Really.

With all their access to everything sexual why would they care what you had to say? Because most of the stuff they are learning from movies and TV and porn are fantasies being sold to them as truths, and when they try and emulate these fantasies in real life they are terribly disappointed and often injured by the experiences. Most of them cannot put words to this. Most of them believe that this is as good as sexuality gets. Most of them silently think something is wrong with them because they are terrified or simply not enjoying it.

I have known many barely eighteen-year-old girls who apathetically say that they are finished with sexuality. Finished. There is a large group of young men so confused by what they see on the Internet, and who have had so many failed in-person sexual experiences that they cannot have real-life relationships. Again, before the age of twenty their sex lives are kaput.

They are thirsty. They will tell researchers they are thirsty. Yet we all know you can bring a horse to water, but you cannot make it ask for advice about sex.

Let's be clear: in this metaphor our teens are horses, thirst is our teens' need for wisdom, wisdom is the quenching beverage and we are the givers of the wisdom. I know nothing about horses, I know tons about teens; therefore I have no idea how you get a stubborn thirsty horse to drink, but I know many ways to get a confused, hurt, embarrassed kid to talk. The most respectful and successful way to talk to kids about sex is to have a conversation about starting a future conversation about sex.

You introduce the topic and then stop it immediately. Do not be tempted to go further. This is a reconnaissance mission to the part of their brain that will listen and heed and drink. It is highly protected like some ancient tomb in an Indiana Jones movie. You must have a map and the secret codes.

Listen carefully:

All this must be said very, very causally, like you could care less how your kid responds. Anything your kid does say must be met with the cool upward nod of the head teens use when saying the word "Dude." Watch them and learn.

Proceed. "So, what's going on in your love life?" (I mean sex life because I doubt they are in love with everyone they are attracted to, but it is more respectful to say love life when talking about sex.) By sex life I mean anything from a crush to a flirt to a physical flirt to hugs to kisses to making out to more making out with fewer clothes on to other stuff that makes us cringe to actual sex. Sex is sexuality and all aspects of it.

Most likely they will say nothing or smile or show their annoyance. That's okay because you have only a few precious moments before they begin the shut- down sequence.

Go for the big question. "You talking to anyone online?" (That's like first base to them.)

Expect some results; a gasp, annoyance, a story, a name, maybe some clue to get you back into the sacred vault. Results occur because you just let them know you have some idea about the joys and horrors of the cyber-sexual world.

Time is ticking. You have about five seconds, so go for it.

"Hey, I know there is some great stuff and some not-so-great stuff on the Internet. I know if I were a teen I'd be curious about it, but there's some messed up stuff on it, too. I'd like to start..."

Three.

"...talking with you..."

Two.

"...about it."

One.

Done! Ears click off, eyes glaze over.

Still, guess what? You got the key to the vault. Well done. You can now access this and help your kid. You didn't go overboard. You didn't judge. You told him you know he's thirsty and that you have water for him. You told her you know there are things that confuse, scare and disappoint her.

14

In just that one moment you've started to alter history. You've pointed out the oasis in the distance.

Let's get them there.

PART II:
ENTER YOUR DESTINATION

He hates me well before he arrives. Only the mentally ill need therapists. His parents need a therapist. He's doing fine.

Sure, he's failing school. Sure, he watches a lot of porn, but his parent's don't know. Sure, he games more than he sleeps, he smokes a ton of pot, and he's had some horrible experiences with girls, but his parents and this shrink don't know that, and won't ever know that. They will only know about his grades and his anger and his apathy.

He's so much harder to catch than the girls because he seldom hears my silent promise of knowing the way out. Getting him to come back to a next session always takes some doing.

I have to prove I know about the things he loves--like the games he plays, the cartoons he watches, the movies he's seen, and the YouTube clips he shares.

Mostly I have sixty ticking minutes to find a spark, a passion, the thing that lifts him out of apathy into fury or fear or joy. It doesn't matter which, just something with a pulse. I have to get him to agree that his goal in life is the same as all of ours, to be happy, to be content, peaceful, connected, and creative. I have to find the boy that until recently was excited about everything.

That boy will lay down his weapons. That boy will play a bit. That boy will listen as I casually point to the way out of his fogged existence.

It would be so much easier if I were a man. We could talk about sexuality now, because that is what he needs, but I have to go so *slowly. It will be so very easy for me to lose him before I ever get to that topic.*

Today we'll talk about South Park and World of Warcraft. We'll laugh at The Ultimate Dog Teaser and I'll show him The Big Slide and he will be blown away. I'll tell him he isn't mentally ill. I'll casually suggest he should come back, to ease his parent's minds, and maybe to get him pointed back to his dreams...to his joy.

Chapter 5:
Know Your Wisdom

(My grammar-check believes this title should be
You're Wisdom. Maybe it's right.)

It might be a good time to get rid of all irritating and fury-inspiring images you might have of your kid right now. Do not recall the week-old Hot Pocket under her bed or the low math grade on his most recent report card; erase the image of over-flowing trash cans and dirty bathroom floors covered with molding towels; ignore the dented bumper, the last minute need for bake-sale cupcakes, and the constant hemorrhage of your wallet. Etch-a-Sketch from your memory the last look your child gave you, which suggested that kid's IQ surpassed your own years ago.

Forget all that. You don't want to figure out what wisdom you have about sex with those images on your mind.

Find a recent good memory with a clear image. You know?...the one when she threw her head back and laughed loud; when he did something incredibly kind and didn't know you were watching; when they were so courageous it brought tears to your eyes. Picture him. Picture her.

What do you hope for that kid's sexual life that will start in her teen years and last until his final breath?

No matter religion, experience, or political bent almost every parent hopes his or her kid will go slow and be safe. That's because kids who go slow have safer and healthier sexual experiences. Kids who start being sexually active in middle school are almost destined to the horrors of high-risk sex, and each school year they postpone, their risk level goes down.

Remember the research says all we have to do is give mindful wisdom about sex to our teens and they will go slower into sexuality.

Mindful means not simply reacting in times of anger, crisis and fear.

Mindful means not just saying the same things our parents said or didn't say.

Mindful parenting on sexuality means you remember your experiences, you know your beliefs, you know what is happening in your teen's world and you communicate this as directly and honestly and respectfully as possible.

Recall that great kid, the one that can bring tears to your eyes: joyful, kind, courageous. For him, for her, let's start exploring the history that has led to your wisdom for that soul.

As Julie Andrew's sang in The Sound Of Music, "Let's start at the very beginning, a very good place to start." Let's start with your experiences of sexuality. Take some time. Go through each question. Write them down or not. Take a holy pause after each question, maybe take a few breaths. Don't speed through these because these are the foundations of your wisdom.

- *What was it like when your body began waking up sexually? How old were you? Do you have any specific memories about this?*
- *What had you thought about sex up to that point?*
- *Where you curious, aroused, confused?*

- *How did your parents handle your sexual awakening? Did they ignore it? Give you advice? Try to control it?*
- *What was your first crush like?*
- *Your first kiss?*
- *Your first make-out session?*
- *Your first time having sex?*
- *How did that all go for you?*
- *How is your sex life now?*
- *How have your spiritual, political and family beliefs influenced and/or conflicted with your sexual experiences?*
- *What experience do you have with the cyber-sexual world?*
- *What are some of your regrets around your sexuality?*
- *What are some of your fondest sexual memories?*

Since many of us have had some sexual assault during our lives it is important to acknowledge the influence an assault may have had both on your experiences and on how you will respond to your child's sexuality. If you don't feel healed in this area, it is one in which guidance can be helpful.

You may find that once you open up to your sexual history more and more memories will start knocking on your door. Let them in because wisdom has need of the whole truth.

It might have been a fun-filled scrapbook you pulled down from the attic or a scary basement scene where zombies come out of nowhere or a bit of both. It doesn't matter because it is all history now. You do not need to tell your child any of this, but you do need to know how you've arrived at your wisdom.

With this newfound wisdom how can you best influence your kid's sexual choices and behavior? There are many factors, from who your kid is to how you present your information to how you parent in general.

Researchers have found that it doesn't matter if you mindfully say wait until marriage or get on birth control, because anything you say mindfully will encourage your kid to slow down and be safer. How long they wait is a huge issue for parents and has far less to do with the actual message as it does with some external factors and the manner in which the parents gave their wisdom. The who and the how.

Who is most likely to have earlier and less safe sex comprises an odd and varied list. They include children conceived out of wedlock, children who mature early (like the side-burned sixth grader and B-cup fifth grader), children whose parents divorce and one or both of them have a sexual awakening, teens in cold relationships with their parents, adolescents who have been sexually assaulted, children who are younger siblings, kids who do poorly in school, and (I love this one) kids who have a lot of pocket money. These don't destine a kid to early sex, but if your kid falls on this list you might be especially mindful and diligent in giving your kid your wisdom (and less cash.)

The amount of influence our wisdom will have has as much to do with what we are saying as how we are saying it. Okay, so we're back to the thirsty horse. We have the water (our newly articulated wisdom), now what? How do we make them drink?

I don't know how to make your kid drink because I don't know your kid. There are many ways to package and deliver your wisdom. In my case, I wrote a book.

You can be direct in short and frequent conversations.

You can watch TV and movies together and talk about the sexuality being portrayed.

You can use moments when they tell you about things occurring with their friends.

You can discuss the media's bombardment of sexual images.

You can tell stories from your youth.

You can ask questions.

You can listen to everything your kid says.

You can be creative. I know a mom and her daughter who used a journal they hid in the piano bench to converse back and forth about sex.

You can give them good books that you have read and agree with.

You can look at websites with good information and point them to the ones you like.

You can let them talk with counselors and doctors and sex education teachers and clergy and aunts and uncles and other adult mentors.

We try everything and notice which things inspire drinking, (horse and water, not the other kind.)

The last part of the how to get them to drink includes every day parenting skills that have been proven to heighten your influence on their sexual behavior (and on all behavior). They include the warmth of your everyday relationship and your ability to monitor their behavior.

Chapter 6:
Know the Temperature

The most dependable thing you can do to ensure your horse/kid will drink the wisdom you have on sexuality is to be in a warm relationship with them, (the kid, not the horse, though I am sure the horse will appreciate it too.)

I love that research on parent/teen health focuses on warmth of relationship because we all know exactly what the opposite of that is...icy. We all know icy. We still remember when our parents became icy; when the temperature of the air dropped like the moment unseen demons arrive in horror movies and breath becomes cold white fog. We know it when our kid scares us or breaks our heart or lets us know just how little control we have over them. We know how our jaws tighten and the blood in our veins freezes and the doors to our hearts slam shut.

We also know warmth. We know when they melt us into puddles of goo; when we take off our armor so we can play in the waves; when our homes glow gold. We know. It is the difference between a calm, deep-voiced navigation system and a high-pitched screech giving you directions.

Habit and stress are the usual culprits for breaking the emotional thermostat in our homes so we feel we cannot regulate the temperature. Stress chills the air, and let's face it, parents and kids are often stressed these days. It seems we never have enough time, money and energy. Stoking the family fireplace just isn't on our To Do list. Warm or cold also has a lot to do with how we were raised. Warm homes beget warm homes. Cold home beget cold homes.

As with wisdom, it takes mindfulness to make things warmer. There are simple ways to warm up a relationship even if your relationship habits are more wintry than summer. Warmth is better, it just is. How many folks vacation in Antarctica compared to some tropical get-a-way? Kids flee cold homes in search of warmth, often into the hot arms of other teens.

But we have to parent them and they are so aggravating!

Please don't think I'm suggesting we must be warm in our relationships 24/7. That just won't happen. In fact, justified icy glares inspired by some dumb decision our kid made are one of the few steady perks of being the parent of a teenager. Still, the temperature of our homes really must be more toaster than freezer even though we are often at crossed purposes with our kids.

This makes me think of the old Looney Toons cartoon in which Ralph E. Wolf and Sam Sheepdog daily battle over their crossed purposes; the wolf must steal the sheep, the sheepdog must protect them. The humor comes when they punch the time-clock in and out each day and lay down their arms. They say things like, "Good Morning, Ralphie," and "See you tomorrow, Sam." They even eat lunch together like old friends.

Parenting teens often feels like that, like we battle all day over our crossed purposes: theirs, to express and test their power and stretch their limits; ours, to give them not only social, moral, and safety wisdom, but boundaries. Yet even though we've fought wickedly the night before, we converse just like regular folks over lunch money and dinner plans the next morning.

These regular moments when we lay down our arms are important. They build in the warmth that must exist in our relationships if we are to smile at the end of our days, knowing we did okay by that kid. (That isn't the outcome the research reports. They focus on teen pregnancy and school performance and drug and alcohol use, but it all comes down to doing okay by our kids, doesn't it?)

It is a prudent exercise to regularly gauge how warm the relationship is. I ask parents and teens what percentage of their waking time together they are warm, what percentage they are neutral and what percentage they are icy. Icy cannot be more than forty percent for any length of time before the relationship begins to suffer from emotional frost bite. Twenty percent or less is better.

When icy begins to do permanent damage to the relationship we have to warm it up. It isn't that hard. It is that important.

Take inventory of what always warms you and your teen's relationship. We all have a list that started when they were young and adorable and warmed our hearts into what seemed like forever-cozy. It could be watching some show regularly. It could be Taco Tuesday or game night or hiking or skiing or making some great dinner or chewy cookies or getting your nails done or fixing a car or traveling or drinking chai or visiting relatives or painting pottery. These are like logs that can stoke the fire to keep us toasty for this long winter of adolescence.

Sometimes the thermostat gets so stuck at temperatures that keep ice cream and hearts hard that the old standbys just won't work. At that time I pull out the big three: fun, food and generosity. These are blasts of hot air that defrost terror and hurt and habit instantly. Keep this list around too. What is always instantly fun? Water fights? A bet? Wrestling? A movie? What food always makes him smile? Soft serve ice cream? A caramel latte? Pizza? Your spaghetti? What small generosity reminds her that, deep down, you like each other? An iTunes card? Good shampoo? Cocoa Puffs?

It is interesting to note that most things that warm relationships make us focus on the present moment. Icy tends to live in the past and the future. Warm is now. When you can let go of past infractions or future worries you have a far warmer home and relationship.

After a particularly emotionally frigid day when my kid was six she came up to ask if she could paint with water-colors. Recalling the previous hours of annoyances I said frostily, "No!" She told me all the reasons it would be alright for her to paint. I heard none of them for I had frostbitten eardrums. "No!" I said again. She then patiently made every reasonable argument for painting, noting its pro-social value, the calming effects of creativity, giving me an hour away from her. Whatever, kid. I said my final "No!"

She began nodding her sweet face in acceptance and said, "Okay...okay...but one day I'll be bigger." She didn't say she'd be older. She said she'd be bigger. Suddenly I remembered the hundreds of hulking teens sitting on my couch because they'd gotten bigger in cold households and now they had control of the thermostat. I caught a glimpse of the future our current sled team was pulling us towards. I vowed to keep the temperature between us at least warm enough for the gold fish to survive in. That should be enough. I remembered her six-year-old words and my vow every time we fought or she hurt my feelings or scared me, and I forced myself to shut the doors to the elements.

Checking the relationship temperature regularly and keeping it warm, or even lukewarm, most of the time can alter our history from the typical exhausted frustration and terror that often marks these years, to the humorous power struggles of Ralph and Sam. (And remember-- Sam wins out over Ralph every time.)

Chapter 7:
Know the Answers to The Four

Kids whose parents monitor their behavior navigate all aspects of adolescence better than kids whose parents do not monitor their behavior.

Who? What? When? Where? (Don't even try Why?) These are The Four. If it is not currently your habit to ask these questions of your child for every moment they are away from you, make it your habit. From the moment of their birth you must know the answers to The Four.

Who? What? When? Where?

Mom? Dad?

They must always have the answers on the tips of their tongues. Always. There should be memo boards or pads of paper filled with the answers to these questions in writing should lawyers need to be involved. All requests for activities should include detailed answers to The Four.

Mandatory. Automatic. Habit. Like covering your mouth before you cough. Like please and thank you. Just do it.

That being said please don't assume you will always get accurate answers to The Four. Frequently The Four inspire a great deal of creative fiction on your teen's part. I did not completely understand this, so after my daughter's ten-thousandth lie I'd become atheistic to the belief I could ever monitor her behavior. Then I realized The

Four are only Part One of the monitoring equation. Intermittent audits are Part Two; a very necessary Part Two.

You audit because your intuition says something's up. You audit because it's been awhile since you checked in on them. You audit to remind them that when they least expect it you will audit them. You audit to keep them on their toes. You audit to keep them as honest as a teen can be.

Auditing includes showing up at events they say they are attending. Auditing is calling the adult they swear is present during parties and sleepovers. Auditing is contacting the teacher they claim marked them absent in error. Auditing is simply, "Just checking the facts, Ma'am."

I am going to admit something that might reduce my credibility. Of all the things that brought me joy as a parent, I think that busting my kid in a lie was one of my favorites. It brought a sense of righteous adventure and excitement like being in a Mission: Impossible movie.

If you do it right you will only have to seriously bust your kid a few times during adolescence, (though I will admit there are some kids who need almost no monitoring and some who demand constant monitoring based on traits that seem to come with them at birth like freckles and eye color). Like a few speeding tickets slow most of us down, a couple of choice stings keep them honest, or honest enough.

A good bust almost always begins with a parental intuition (or a really obvious lie by the kid.) It might start as you're driving home from a movie on some weekend night. This is novel for you because your kid has just gotten old enough to be out without you on weekend nights, which means you now have evenings to go out like you did before children. As you drive you start to think how much you are enjoying your freedom. This makes you recall who the freedom is from. Then you suddenly remember the moment your kid left the house this evening; how her make-up was heavier than usual or his cologne was so strong your eyes burned when he hugged you good-bye. Hugged me good-bye? He never does that. Then, little bits of information you ignored begin to form the thought that your kid is not who, what, when and where he said he was.

You grab the phone and speed-dial that kid's number.

My kid was easy to bust because if I called and she was where she was supposed to be she answered with an angry hushed tone, "What?" If she was not where she was supposed to be her voice was several octaves higher and louder and happier than usual.

"Hi Mom. What's up?"

Then I began laying the foundations for the ultimate bust, because the tangled web is far more fun than the single lie.

"Where are you?" I ask carefully taking in the background traffic sounds coming from the receiver.

Again, if she was where she was supposed to be she'd say indignantly, "At Jenny's." But the liar daughter talks fast and gives details that would make a used car salesman blush. "I'm at Jenny's. She has a really nice house. You'd like it. It's way out in Fruita. It's pretty big and they have a pool table, but I'm bad at pool so we aren't playing."

"Who's there?"

"Just me and Jenny and Jenny's mom. She's really cool. You'd like her. I think she knows some people you know." Now that she's on a roll I don't even have to ask her any questions. "We're watching this TV show. We should rent it. I think we can get it on Netflix. And Jenny's mom got us this pizza. It's pretty good, but not as good as Pahgre's and it had green peppers on it and I really don't like green peppers, but I tried to eat them to be polite, but I really don't like them so I picked the rest of them out."

I can't tell you the joy that is coursing through me as I listen to her rant.

She finally pauses.

My turn.

"Hey," I say playfully. "Send me a picture of you with Jenny's mom and that pizza box."

Silence. Well, almost. She is thinking so hard how she might be able to get out of this that I can hear a slight grinding noise. When she realizes there is no way out of this lie she decides her only chance is volume.

She screams into the phone, "Okay, so I'm not at Jenny's, but that's because...."

Oh no, there is no excuse for that whopper. I stop her cold. "No! Get home right now. You have fifteen minutes." Click. I hang up that phone before she starts to talk again.

There is really no place more than fifteen minutes from your home. This is one of the many odd facts in quantum physics.

I go to the front porch and begin to swing like a cat twitching its tail. The colder the temperature the better to help rev me into self-righteous indignation. She drives home desperately thinking of how to get out of this check-mate.

She arrives fifteen minutes and twelve seconds later, just late enough to prove her soon-to-be-destroyed power.

I catch her eyes, then walk into the house because no one, especially a child therapist, needs their neighbors to hear what is about to transpire.

I walk directly to the stairs and climb four. I need a height advantage that accurately represents my moral superiority. As I climb these stairs I begin to feel a gathering of other parents' souls cheering me on, for parents seldom have such clear moral ground with teens. I imagine their wispy figures filling my living room; waiting, watching, supporting.

The kid comes in screaming. I can't blame her. She really only has volume and guilt against my arsenal of God-is-on-my-side

31

bombs. There have been times when guilt has slowed me down, but not for an infraction this mighty.

What follows is a battle of two powerful women; one older, one busted. It is like the slow motion fight between Scar and Simba in The Lion King. She slashes me with reasons why she has to lie to me. She claims I do not listen; I do not trust her; and the big one, the one that sometimes works with me, she claims I like my clients more than I like her.

I counter with, "You lied." Bam! "You lied." Bam! "You lied." For the final blow, the winning blow, I say, "My clients don't lie to me." (Okay it doesn't sound like a winning blow, but it worked.)

She falters like Scar and falls. Defeated, she slinks to her room realizing she cannot get away with lying. She simply can't. This defeat will keep her from many dangerous situations and sexually compromising possibilities.

As she leaves to ponder the depths of her defeat I, like Simba, begin my victory walk up Pride Rock (the stairs to my room) in extreme slow motion with a crescendo of The Lion King theme song. My fellow parents, gathered below, cheering me on.

Busts allow for some good battles to let off steam. They allow kids to be naughty without life-altering consequences. They allow us to be right. They remind them that they are being monitored and, oddly, this increases our influence over their sexuality.

PART III:
CAUTION...ROUGH ROAD AHEAD

We're there. One session or seven, it doesn't matter. We're there.

They are ready to talk, they are ready to hear.

She wants to tell me about the boys asking; about being terrified; about not understanding as she pulls off her shirt and snaps a photo of herself. How she hesitates, then looks at the photo of her girl's face atop that woman's body; how thrilled, scared, proud she feels; how she pushes the Send button and the photo of her body enters the raging river of cyber-space, now completely out of her control. Without words she begs me to understand, to not judge and to have some answers to calm her fears and guilt.

He doesn't ask or tell. There is just a time when I know I can tell him that I know a lot of boys having a hard time with their sexual lives; that porn is hard to resist; that they are pressured to ask girls for photos and sex talk online, to do sexual stuff quickly with girls in person or they suffer the consequences of being called gay. He stares at the ground as I talk fast. He looks up briefly when I finish. His face is blank as he decides.

The younger kid tells me of stumbling upon porn either as they search for something innocent or when some older kids encourage them to watch it. I can hardly bare to look them as they relive the moment they saw hard-core porn for the first time without a smooth-voiced GPS giving them warning. I can see a close-up of their eyes, their curious faces transforming in slow motion from eager to confused to horrified to hardened; the true transformation of soul to zombie. I can't erase it.

I must silently say to myself over and over, "Inhale. Accept what is. Assess the consequences. Address them with honesty, courage and wisdom. Exhale."

Chapter 8:
Accepting and Assessing Internet Porn
in Their Lives

Basically porn began a zillion years ago as a product for men who wanted a little variety, fantasy and naughtiness in their lives in a fairly safe manner. Photos, magazines, film clips and eventually feature length movies had images of beautiful naked women in provocative poses that inferred, "I am ready for some whoopee!" Its main purpose was to provide arousal material for these men.

Over the years the porn film industry grew. Mostly for men, these films were available to purchase at adult book stores, viewed in peep-type shows and in X-rated theaters.

The formula for the films was always the same. A chance encounter occurred between the lead male(s) and some beautiful woman(women) who was either crazy with sexual want or acting like she didn't have any sexual want even though she was, indeed, crazy with sexual want. This led to a quick sexual experience. The sex was mechanical in movement, lacked any eye contact or genuine connection, and was often somewhat degrading to the woman, but that was okay because she loved it. By the end of the sexual encounter all parties were very happy and smoking cigarettes.

Even though these films stimulated men with their fantasy themes, most men had already had actual sex and did not believe the film depicted true sexuality. It was like watching I Dream of

Jeannie; men might have liked the idea of their wives being beautiful, scantily clothed and easily banished to a bottle, but they knew real marital relationships were simply not like that.

The porn feature film industry was highly successful, but one had to go to a porn theater or adult sex shop in person and many chose to avoid such public viewings and purchases.

Then the Internet arrived where one could access porn anonymously from the safety and comfort of one's own home. Again, it was mainly adults who already had sexual experience that watched early Internet porn because it had to be purchased with credit cards. Also, the family computer was large and heavy and often housed in a communal room like the home office or the breakfast nook. It was far from private.

Over the past ten years Internet connecting devices have become small and mobile. Hackers and software engineers have yielded to the market's desire for unfettered and private access to all sites. Websites have found that more money can be made from advertising than charging per view.

Porn is now free, not easily traced by family members and can be viewed privately anywhere.

The porn industry has boomed, to say the least, with profits over $15 billion dollars a year. For every four hundred movies made in Hollywood, eleven thousand porn films are made.

As the porn industry boomed, the need for more and more novel material has encouraged producers to make the films more aberrant, abusive and unrealistic. This obviously has some consequence for adults who view these films, but folks with real life sexual experiences are usually able to distinguish porn-inspired sex from non-porn-inspired sex. They do know this is fantasy.

As Internet porn became openly accessible to adults, children and teens were able to kick that door open too. Yet they have no sexual experience. What they see they believe and attempt to model as if it were The Idiot's Guide to Sex.

They start watching Internet porn around the age of eleven. Ten years ago if, as a therapist, I found out an eleven-year-old had access to pornography I would have reported it as child abuse, because back then we knew the negative effects those images would have on that's child's mental health and sexual development.

Today if I called my local Child Abuse Hotline because an eleven-year-old has access to Internet porn it would be like me calling the plumber about a leaky faucet just as a tsunami engulfed my town.

Again, adults may have all sorts of issues with porn, but they rarely think porn sex is what real sex is like. They don't really believe that a bunch of guys might go hiking in the woods with their Saint Bernard pulling a Keg-O-Rator, and happen to bump into two hugely breasted women who have just been attacked by a bear, and that all the bear did was rip off their shirts and bras, which somehow left the women highly aroused and ready for anything.

Probably not.

That's a funny example, using an old-school type of porn scenario. Our kids don't get to see much of that. They get harder core porn scenarios like the ones where a very young woman is penetrated by a multitude of men. She simply can't get enough of them. She's left exhausted and humiliated as the conquering men pretend she is nothing. But no worries, because she really had a great time even though any real life woman would be physically shredded. That is the kind of porn they are watching, and even that one is tame compared to most. I just don't have the stomach to describe the worst of them. That is the model they believe.

Mom? Dad?

The main consequences come from teens' inability to distinguish porn-inspired sex from non-porn-inspired sex. Porn teaches them six myths that they end up imitating when they become sexually active.

37

The six myths are:

Sex is anonymous: It doesn't matter who the bodies are. It doesn't matter if you are attracted to them or them to you. It is best if the person is not real to you; has no feelings, family, cares, soul, future or physical limits.

Sex is fast: Once the decision has been made to have sex, intercourse occurs. There is no kissing or caressing, no unfolding, no allowing arousal to get the body ready because porn teaches us that the human body is always ready for hard core sex; male and female, we are always at-the-ready.

Sex is disconnected: There is no connection other than physical during the sexual act. No eyes meet. Bodies are not usually positioned facing towards each other. There are no smiles or moments where soul meets soul, friend meets friend, lover meets lover. Remember, it doesn't matter who is entering you. It does not matter who has taken you into their bodies.

Sex degrades women: The themes of porn movies are almost always degrading and/or abusive to women. They are pummeled, slapped and choked; they are mocked and discarded. They are assumed stupid and without worth. But the important message of porn is that this does not matter because women love this degradation and abuse. It turns them on to no end. It is all part of the fun.

Women are always ready: Sexy girls are always ready for sex; anytime, anyplace, with anyone, and in any way. They don't care. They just want sex at all times. Their bodies require no time or touch for arousal.

Porn sex is a blast: At the end of the film everyone has had a great time. Everyone is happy and satisfied and content.

It is my experience that girls do not enjoy porn and watch far less porn than boys. (Remember the average teen boy watches porn about twenty minutes a day.) Though most teen girls have seen porn, they report that they don't enjoy it. Across the board, girls say the same thing about porn, "Those women aren't having any fun. They are so faking it." Though the porn stars bounce and beg and scream "Harder", it is evident to most females that the actresses are detached from what is happening to their bodies, they are pretty messed up and they seem to be in physical pain.

So, if girls don't like porn, if they don't believe the actresses are enjoying it, how can they possibly be influenced by it?

Currently, most girls who are not given mindful wisdom about sex are getting their modeling through sexually explicit movies and TV where attraction and relationship is everything. It takes a good three-quarters of most romance movies to get to the first kiss. TV series can tease us for seasons before that first kiss. It is almost the opposite for porn.

So where does it all go wrong? At the moment of a kiss the sex then happens about as quickly as the sex in porn. Kiss, kiss, clothes ripped off, bodies on top of bodies, squirming, spooning after. (There is no spooning in porn.) Really, it takes about two minutes from the kiss to the spooning in TV and movies.

So, from a first kiss, boys and girls believe in the same time line. Quick. Bodies always ready.

From there, the porn model trumps. Once they are sexual, the boys (and I mean the good boys, the kind boys, the nice boys, our boys) imitate the porn they watch daily. They detach and get 'er done.

The girls are playing out the deep romance and the boys are getting 'er done. So the dear and fun attraction that began with a sweet kiss takes a wicked turn and becomes a bad porn scene.

Both the boys and the girls feel awkward, disconnected and a little sick. The boys question whether they did something wrong. The girls often feel injured. But, they just did what they'd seen both porn and movie stars do happily again and again. And so, our kids smile and brag. They deny injury and insult.

Then they do it again and again. Few teen relationships last past a few sexual encounters. They move on. They get more detached with each sexual encounter. They deny their deep disappointment.

Watch a few videos on college Spring Breaks. You'll see drunken kids acting like porn stars. They act like having random sex with any and all of their tanned peers is great. Watch the beginning of *The Social Network* where beautiful female students are shipped to a Harvard frat house. The girls quickly strip down to their bra and panties and dance and make out with each other to entertain the boys. It is assumed they hook up sexually with these future leaders.

So maybe this generation is merely more sexually aware and free from repression than we are. Are we just moralizing because we're frustrated and jealous?

Nope.

Hook-up sex, drunken and porn-inspired, isn't good and does not lead to a healthy sex life. Only eighteen percent of the young women have orgasms in such encounters. (No duh, girls have been faking it forever, right?) But here's the other truth no one speaks of, only forty-two percent of the young men orgasm during such sex. Forty-two percent. Porn-inspired sex is sloppy, unsatisfying and humiliating. Girls in college who are sexually active with more than one partner a year experience depression. With each new partner her depression level goes up.

Most of our teens' first visual models of sex comes from Internet porn or sexually explicit TV and movies. Wise directions are necessary to combat the obvious negative repercussions on their sexual choices and behaviors.

Chapter 9:
Cyber Sexing/Sexting

Sexting and cyber-sex are virtual sexuality. Sexting is a term used mainly for sexually explicit talk or photos or videos exchanged through texting. Cyber-sex is the same only the exchange occurs on the Internet. In both, sexual acts are talked about, sexual photos or videos are sent, and real time sexual chatting or videos are exchanged. They are sexual encounters without another's physical presence.

Because it is cyber we often discount it as not really occurring or not being influential. Because it is cyber we judge it as nasty and dirty and bad. The truth is, (are you ready?) it is real sexuality. It is really occurring. It is really affecting everyone engaging in it, including (and maybe especially) our kids. It can be as sweet or as pornographic as any skin to skin sexuality.

Sexuality is sexuality and there is joy and risk in all sexual encounters. In the cyber world our bodies are safe from assault, STI and pregnancies. Our hearts are buffered by miles of airwaves. Certainly. On the other hand, a make-out session in real life has no recorded proof that can be sent over those airwaves. An exposed breast can't be distributed by a bragging partner to all his buddies. An erotic moment won't influence colleges, future in-laws and job opportunities.

Cyber-sex and sexting are easier and engaged in more frequently than in-person sexuality. After all, it can be anonymous, there is little risk to the ego if one is rejected, and we can troll many potential partners; whereas it takes a great deal of energy and exposure to connect with a partner whose breath, minty or bad, you can smell.

The myths and rules of porn fit well with cyber-sex and sexting worlds. One can play out porn inspired sex online in a way that is very difficult in real life. All the myths work. One can be anonymous, wickedly fast, disconnected, degrading and abusive; one can act sexy even when confused and hurt; and one can deny the feelings and humanity of another that is more difficult when eyes are meeting eyes.

One just needs to get 'er done in the cyber world.

Here' a typical teen sexting or cyber-sexual conversation:

"Hey wassup?"

"Not much, wassup with you?"

"I think you're hot."

"LOL." (Stands for "Laughing out loud", but in this context it usually means "I don't know what to say, I sure hope you stop there.")

"Send me a picture of your tits" (or any nude body part we usually cover with some sort of undergarment) or "Let's have cyber-sex" or "DTF?" (Stands for "Down to F_ _ k?" without the blanks.)

I know you are thinking, "No way. No one would get to that request that fast." Believe me when I say the above interaction is probably two exchanges longer than most cyber-sex and sexting requests. That seems fast. Fast as....maybe porn?

It has become the new pressure for boys to gain such commodities as nude photos and sexually explicit texts from girls. They collect these on flash drives, like they used to collect Pokémon,

Yu-Gi-Oh, and baseball cards in albums. They send them out to other boys. They trade them.

These boys ask strangers and best girlfriends alike. They forget that these girls are their friends, future co-workers, wives and fellow human beings. It's a problem. (These harmful requests can obviously come from girls or from same-sex friends though the majority comes from boys to girls.)

Please know that most teens have had these interactions from the time they are in middle school. The requests are quick and direct.

Girls almost always say "No" to boys' initial requests. They really do. They feel scared and confused and guilty. They also feel a bit important and sexy and naughty. The boys ask again and again and again and again. They act adorable. They act hurt by the rejections. They promise love and devotion. They promise not to show anyone. They get mean. They threaten. They are relentless. RELENTLESS.

Most surveys show that about a third of teenage girls eventually engages in some sex talk or send a photo. They regret it from the moment they push SEND. Once they push SEND they are completely exposed. At any moment the recipient can send that exchange or photo or video to anyone they choose. It can end up anywhere. It can destroy not only their current reputations, but also their future reputations since a cyber-history lasts forever.

They are also exposed legally. Most teens do not truly believe their legal risk. At least not until they push SEND. At that point they recall the lectures by adults on the legal charges being given girls and boys who push SEND. They are all at risk for getting a felony charge of distributing child pornography. It gives them a sex offense charge that cannot be removed from their records. This means as they grow up they have to inform all prospective employers that they are sex offenders, and that they must register with law enforcement every time they move to give them their new address so the good citizens of the town are aware of their locations. This is seriously the current legal ramification for sexting and cyber-sexing. It has seriously not occurred to many teens. It is seriously the wrong punishment for impulsive teens to be treated like adult predators. It ruins lives.

Very few kids think about any of this until they push SEND. Then it is too late.

The reality is that cyber-sex and sexting will be as much a part of our children's and grandchildren's lives as football games and first kisses and burgers and Coke. If we can discourage the myths of porn as the main influence of their cyber-sexuality and their real life sexuality, it might just turn out fine.

Chapter 10:
Huh. What Do We Do About Internet Porn, Cyber-sex and Sexting?

Over the past two and a half decades of counseling teens I have developed an important skill. I use it when they tell me something horrible and double-dare me not to look shocked. Over the years I have trained myself to become calmer the more overwhelmed I am. So as they tell me about some terribly unsafe thing they've done or some trauma that has occurred, my breath deepens, my heart rate slows, and my face dead-pans to the look of runway models. I look as though nothing fazes me.

And then I say, "Huh."

Huh is a secret code that scrambles the words in my head so teens cannot hear them. As my mind screams: *you did what, they asked you for what, you saw what*, they only hear the very innocuous "Huh." This buys me time to regroup so that my first response does not silence them. It buys me the time I need to go through my list of what to do.

As you help your kid navigate through all this, use the gift of *Huh.* You'll seem like a very cool like character in a spy movie who calmly sips martinis even though danger looms everywhere. You'll get to seem like you have all the wisdom they need, and hopefully you will.

Besides generously using "Huh" or its unfazed persona, you also begin having the important conversations. As discussed at the end of Chapter Four you start these difficult conversations by announcing you will be having them in the future. This gives you and your kid time to prepare.

Then have short conversations. I need to say this again. Have short conversations. Talk about one or two points at a time, not everything. Choose the points you will discuss based on what your kid has told you, anything you've discovered, or what you suspect they need.

Point One: Tell your kid you know that they have access to porn. Tell them you know about cyber-sex and sexting. Tell them you suspect that they and/or their friends have experienced these or might in the future. Tell them that you think they need information about these potentially damaging influences.

Point Two: The main reason kids don't ask us for help with problems arising from cyber-sex and sexting is because they will share nothing that might risk their technology being taken away from them. This is difficult, because the first thing we want to do when we hear a kid is watching porn or being harassed or has sent some nude photo is to take the phone and computer and throw them into the bottom of the ocean. Though that may seem like the best solution, it will only lead to them sneaking and telling us nothing. Remember, they can buy Go Phones for less than the cost of a week's worth of caramel lattes. Therefore, you must tell them you know these things might happen. You can tell them that you won't take away their technology if they choose to talk to us about the issues, and use them responsibly. You tell them you will help them deal with the problems.

Point Three: If you decide to focus on porn, start by telling them that porn is fantasy. Tell them that our bodies and souls do not work like that in real life. Tell them that there is a difference between porn-inspired sex and non-porn-inspired sex. Tell them that porn-inspired sexuality will not lead to love and romance and happiness.

Point Four: Go over the six myths.

Point Five: Tell them that because so many of their peers and girlfriends and boyfriends have seen porn they will need to help educate them about the effects of porn or it will seep into their romances and sexual encounters.

Point Six: You can tell them what real sexuality is like. Tell them that we do much better if we know the other person, if we slowly unfold to sexuality. Tell them that if they go slowly they will be safer and healthier and happier. Tell them about all the fun steps from a kiss to intercourse; the steps missed completely by porn. Tell them you hope they play on first and second base. Research teen fiction and non-fiction books, websites and educational material that talks about good and healthy sexual development and progression. Give your child the ones that are in line with your values, beliefs and philosophies.

Some of the points below relate to requests for pictures and sexual chatting. I use the examples of boys requesting from girls although this clearly occurs boy to girl, girl to boy, boy to boy and girl to girl. The information works in all these situations.

Point Seven: If you are talking with a boy, tell him that you know about sexting and cyber-sex. You need to remind him about the negative consequences of requesting sexually explicit photos and conversation. You need to remind boys to be kind, to remember these girls are their friends and future partners. You need to remind them girls are not to be collected and shared and discounted like the women in porn. You need to teach them to say, "Not cool, Dude" when someone sends them a compromising photo of a real life girl.

Point Eight: If you are talking with a girl about cyber-sex and sexting, you need to help her learn how to deal with these requests. First, you should acknowledge that there is something exciting and grown-up about the whole thing. Parents of teens who have participated in sexting and cyber-sex are constantly screaming, "Why didn't she just say 'No'?" *This should not be!* Ah well, it is. It is hard to say "No", especially if the boy is making them feel grown-up or afraid or beautiful.

Point Nine: Both boys and girls need to know that these cyber-interactions are not private and might harm them in the future. They need to know the possible legal consequences for these interactions.

Point Ten: Both boys and girls really need to know how to say "No" long before they are cyber-talking to someone. Let them know that because of how quickly cyber-sexual exchanges occur, they need to say "No" or draw boundaries at the beginning of a cyber-conversation or as soon as someone crosses a sexual line. They do well to say upfront things like "I am waiting until..." "I don't cyber-sex so if you ask I will just block you."

Point Eleven: Blocking inappropriate requesters is the easiest and most permanent "No" a teen can use. All chat rooms and social networks and phones have simple ways to block others from contacting them. Help your teen find the ways to block offending others from their cyber-world. It works well for people they have only met on-line.

Point Twelve: Adults need to know that there is a great deal of social pressure not to block someone they know in real life. It is a huge social slap to be blocked from someone's phone or social networking page. The most effective "No" when blocking teens they know in real life is to use their parents as excuses. They can blame their parents' monitoring skills. They can say that their parent reads all their texts so they can't talk about sex. I have encouraged parents and kids to have an agreement that when someone crosses the sexual comfort line the kid can enlist their parents to help them get rid of the inappropriate "friend." Parents and kids agree the kid can tell sexually demanding cyber-friends that their parents are insanely protective and controlling, and that they check their texts, email, social networks and chat histories all the time. They can tell these cyber-requesters that their parents report sexually inappropriate contact to the police, even if they don't. I know a daughter/Dad duo that joins forces when she gets an inappropriate text from a boy. She takes a picture of her dad looking angry. Then she sends the picture with a message like "OMG...my dad just grabbed my phone and read your text. I told him I'd block you if he wouldn't come after you. Sorry."

Point Thirteen: Another easy "No" involves making the inappropriate requests public. I love to encourage girls who are getting cyber sexual requests to simply forward it to all her friends, because most of these requesters are sending requests out with rapid-fire. That way, all the girls who have gotten requests from him realize he is just playing them all. He frequently uses the same words and methods. Girls find this very unattractive. So they forward the requests, effectively stopping him, rather than sending him a photo that he sends off to all his buddies. It gives the girls the upper hand. It gives a social consequence to that boy and all other boys trolling for cyber-sexual interactions with their female peers.

Point Fourteen: Teens also need very specific ways to say "No" to the porn-quick sexual advances in real life; flesh to flesh. As with cyber-sexuality, because it goes so quickly from a slight attraction to very sexual encounters, (a diagonal run from first base to third without even touching second) they need to set their boundaries ahead of time and have words of refusal on their tips of their tongues. I know powerful teens that set the limits in texts before the date. I know happy and confident teens who tell the object of their affection that they are kissers and only kissers. Practice with your teen ways to say "No". I find some kids openly appreciate this. Some kids moan and groan, but the next time they get a request they have the words and the skills they need.

49

Some classic refusal lines:

  I only kiss.

  I am not comfortable with that.

  I don't know you that well.

  Stop.

  That's too much.

  Gotta go.

  Dude, what are you doing? Absolutely not.

  Hey...I meant it when I said I only want to kiss.

  I really like you, but let's go a lot slower.

Point Fifteen: The absolute best way for your kids to say "No" is to learn how to tell the requester just how the request made them feel. They need to be able to tell them why they are choosing to block them from their phones and computers and lives. This way, other misled teens, most of them really nice kids, will get feedback.

You can help your kid by asking how the request made him/her feel. They will often not have the words. This is a great time to help them learn how to identify what they are really feeling about all this stuff. Words like *confused, angry, scared, bullied, pressured, freaked-out, messed-up, betrayed,* and *used* might help. Help them put words to concepts like I really liked you and now I can't trust you, and I was having fun talking to you and now I never want to talk to you again. Telling the kid who wrote them inappropriate sexual requests that they talked with their parents about it will usually scare that kid off.

Since so many kids are unconsciously using porn as their sexual model, encourage your kids to educate each other whenever they can. I know girls who, once they have this information, say to the boys something like, "By what you just asked me to do, I think maybe you are watching a lot of porn and you think that is really what sex is about. It isn't. You just went from saying "Hey" to asking for things you should only ask someone you know really well. You scared me, and now I don't ever want anything to do with you. You might want to think about how you do these things because you seemed really nice before all that."

Point Sixteen: As they get older, watch movies with teen sexual themes then talk about them. Most current romantic comedies will provide perfect opportunities. It is sometimes easier to talk about a fictitious sexual situation than a real one because parents will be less fearful and angry, and teens will be able to talk without guilt and defense. There is good research that shows watching TV with your teens and talking about it is one of the most effective parenting tools we have. It is significantly better than allowing them to watch TV alone.

Point Seventeen: We go to the phone store every time we've earned an up-grade or our phone gets laundered or some new phone promises a more joyful life. How about taking a trip for your teen? Go and get educated on how to block calls, how to report harassing perpetrators, how to monitor your child's contacts, texting hours, and the content of their words and photos and videos. Know what sorts of controls you do have...and then, of course, exercise them.

Go home and educate your kid.

Point Eighteen: Finally, unplug them by 10 at night. They need to sleep. Let's give them a rest between 10 p.m. and 6 a.m.. Let's let them dream for eight hours. Encourage other parents to make this a norm, like breakfast in the morning. Sexual predators are out combing the Internet between 10 and 6; teens are plotting nighttime adventures between 10 and 6, crazy teen gossip explodes between 10 and 6; most porn is watched between 10 and 6; most cyber-sex and sexting occur between 10 and 6. Ignore their whining. Take the phone and the music pod and the gaming system and the laptop. May the groans of unplugged youths be our nation's 10 p.m. chime.

PART III: POINTS OF INTEREST

(Places a little out of the way, but important to the journey.)

At some point their parents will come in for guidance. "Without the kid," I insist, because I will need to tell them everything about Internet porn and sexting and cyber-sex, and like their children, their faces will transform from attentive to bewildered to horrified. They will need to rant.

They will need to yell that their children should be able to go on an adventure into the Internet without being mustard-gassed by porn; that they should be able to flirt and meet and greet without predators and peers alike exploiting them; that they should be able to mature and slowly try on sexuality like a prom dress without being injured. They will need to scream "This should not be" until they are hoarse.

And then we will begin their education on how to help their children navigate this cyber world. I will encourage them to put words to their wisdom. I will remind them that their children's happiness is always North.

As the dust settles their eyes and minds will clear and questions will begin to spring from their lips; questions about their younger children, about masturbation and abstinence, about the nasty gossip that seems to influence their kid's sexuality, about how difficult it is for fathers to talk to their sons.

These are the same questions parents ask again and again. I smile and pull the appropriate essay from the file drawers in my mind.

Chapter 10:
The Wee Ones

For those souls who have yet to stumble upon porn while browsing the Internet, for those who have not been asked for sexual photos or videos or interactions, for them, the under-elevens, the less-than-techno savvy, the very young or the very lucky, there is great opportunity to immunize, to fit them for protective glasses, to give them driving directions.

When we have this information before our kids have these experiences we are in the driver's seat. These kids have the opportunity to enjoy the wonders of the Internet with far fewer high-risk consequences.

First, foremost, there must be one very explicit rule governing all cyber-connected devices: there is zero privacy online. We will look at their browsing histories. We will know their passwords to all social networking. We will randomly look at their texting histories.

The mindset is not "Here are the keys to heaven and hell, to connection and exploitation alike, have fun Sweetie." No, the mindset is "These are amazing tools. You need to be aware of their potential for connecting and research and exploring, and you need to know the safety rules." As with all of our child's activities we will know who, what, when and where, and we will audit.

Get technological assistance when (there is no if here) their technological skills at evading your watchful eyes outsmart your own.

Teach them that there are cyber issues that can be harmful to them. Educate them on the power of visual images on the brain; how it is hard to get these images out of the brain once there, how they can influence their behavior, and how they will model these actions whether they want to or not. Give them examples we have noticed in their lives like when they couldn't sleep due to some scary image they saw in a movie or on TV; or how they try to imitate people in real life or on the screen who they think are cool.

Tell them we really want them to talk to us if they happen to see anything that scares or confuses them; tell them we will not be angry. (Otherwise they won't share this information and, really, it is not their fault, they will just be lured like fish to hooks.)

Teach them refusal skills. Show them how to block anyone that bothers them or makes them feel uncomfortable. A block is the best "No" out there. Explain that there are millions of people on the Internet and, just like in real life, some of them are nice and some are mean, some lie, some want things from them, and some will try to get them into trouble. Balance this by pointing out how, like in real life, some are fun and interested in the same things they are and can add to their lives.

Show them how to report inappropriate messages to chat room and social networking sites' monitoring systems.

Explain to them why they must never, ever give personal information like where they live, their phone numbers, their school, etc., to people they have only met online.

Explain to them why they must never meet someone they met online without you present. Tell them unsafe people will not want to meet their parents.

Talk with them about their cyber world the way you would about their real life world. Do not discount the cyber world as a fictitious part of their lives. Ask them about and be as interested in their answers as you are in their answers about real life. Ask them who they are talking to. Find out about their cyber friends the same way you would find out about their real friends. Ask what their cyber friends are interested in. Get excited about the things your kid is exploring on the Internet. Have them show you the sites they love. Tell them if you are concerned about anything or anyone just as you would in real life. Honor their cyber-world.

Put limits on their technology. Always turn theirs (and yours) off during meals. Set time limits that are appropriate to the amount of free time they have each day and to their need of real life play, thought, chores, homework and interactions. Give them time to use their own imaginations. Turn off all cyber-connecting technology at night. Model all this for them because if we can't turn it off they will never be able to turn it off.

These helpful hints work for kids of all ages, but it is very hard to reign in kids' use of technology once they have been using it without rules and with complete privacy. It then becomes a task of breaking a wild horse. So if that is where we find ourselves, remember (again, I know very little about horses)--be kind and go slow and explain in a calm, and soothing way why we are changing the rules.

Chapter 11:

Mast Herb Ace Shun

There are topics we simply don't talk about, like what occurs between ourselves and the toilet in the morning after our cup of coffee. It is just in bad taste because it is no one's business but our own.

Unless...we need to. Then we might have to speak of the unspeakable with a wise soul.

Because teens have unlimited opportunity to access porn, cyber-sexuality, explicit texting, photos, videos, and exchanges, perhaps their hands will be finding their nether regions and explosions the likes of the Fourth of July will occur.

So, is there a problem? Do we mention it? Is it any of our business? Do we have strong thoughts or beliefs for or against it? Do we have different thoughts about boys and girls engaging in such? Do we want to skip this chapter entirely?

Whether you talk about it with your teen or not is up to you. I do think if you are going to be mindful about your wisdom it would be good to know what you think, believe and feel about self-pleasure (a much nicer term that that other one). Teen sexuality and self-pleasure do go hand-in-hand (pun definitely intended).

Did you? You know...did you? Do you? Did anyone talk to you about it? Were you told it was natural or aberrant or sinful? In my youth, boys were told tell-tale signs like hair growing on their palms or blindness were the fate of self-pleasuring boys, kind of like the myth that a chemical was put in all public pools that created bright a bright red hue around you if you peed in the pool. Like pool peeing, these threats were probably tested for accuracy.

There is some research that might help in your decision-making. The health benefits of self-pleasure are that it provides a healthy outlet for people who choose to abstain, it allows people to be familiar with their sexual bodies, it alleviates stress, aids in sleep and enhances self-esteem. (I got this directly off of a pamphlet in my doctor's office.)

There are some religions that have very strong mandates against self-pleasure, and I assume they give parenting advice on the topic.

If you want your kid to delay sex, especially if you want your kid to abstain until marriage (at the average age of 27) I suggest you know how you feel about things to do with the very, very (shall I say it again?) VERY strong urge to drive that Ferrari. It is only fair.

If you choose to address this topic here are some tips:

Be brief. This is not a topic you need to discuss at length or frequently. One dose should last a lifetime.

I really think this topic is best discussed same sex...so woman to girl; man to boy.

It is difficult to start this discussion. I use words like, "Do you know how your body works sexually?"

This topic is often easier learned through other expert sources. Parents who want the kid to have information can give them books (I like the self-pleasure section in *Our Bodies; Ourselves.*) Great information can be found in pamphlets at the pediatricians' offices and sex education web sites. These are usually teen friendly and often quite humorous. They address the topic in a straightforward manner that parents often cannot. The fact that you researched these, found the ones you like and are aligned with your morals and beliefs shows your kid that you think this is an important topic and that you are respecting his or her privacy about this topic.

Humor helps. There is a great line in *Bridesmaids* where the mother of three adolescent boys says of their constant self-pleasure, "The other day I found a blanket that broke in half. It literally broke in half."

Chapter 12:
Drama and Gossip

It used to be that teens who gossiped all day and used information, true or false, as power, as status, as money in the bank, comprised a small percent of the teen world. In teen books of old, the gossip-spreading kids were always bullies in a sea of non-bullies and they always got theirs in the end because gossipy, high drama kids are not happy. It always came back on them because they destroy any sense of trust and friendship and fun and group dynamics.

Back then, if a gossip came into my office I suspected his/her parents were gossips. We really do influence our kids and gossip transfers from parent to kid like the love or hate of Miracle Whip. So, mean-spirited, gossipy parents often created mean-spirited gossipy kids, but that was just a small percent of the families out there.

I mean, by and large Americans are respectful, kind and truthful, right? We know how to keep a secret? We don't spread information that could be harmful or untrue? We create environments that encourage us to be smart and creative and innovative. These allow us to be adventurous and courageous. All these things allow us the freedom that is our country's greatest inherited gift, leading to happiness, right?

Gossip undermines freedom. It makes us paranoid and scared to put ourselves out there. It undermines our confidence. It makes us shut up and distrust and try fewer things and think smaller thoughts. It cages us.

So ten years ago gossip/drama parents equaled gossip/drama kids and that accounted for a small percent of the population.

Then I began to notice a much larger group of drama queens and gossips appearing. This occurred when reality shows began to dominate television. Socially and morally inept people screamed and blamed and spewed private matters at each other on national TV. The old values of respect and listening were thrown out the window. Like porn, these shows are far from reality. Reality is kind of blissfully dull. A conflict between two normal citizens has little television viewing value. In fact, reality shows give psychological assessments to possible contestants and chose those with Personality Disorders because they are so much more fun to watch.

With the advent of reality television shows, gossip and drama spread from the poorly parented to the majority of kids. Enter 24/7 news shows (conservative and liberal alike.) Somehow that dull hour-a-day of news we used to watch to keep informed about our community, a little about our world, and mostly for the weather and sports turned into the twenty-four hour circus that it is today. Twenty-four hours. Hard news will not draw an audience for more than an hour. No. Only gossip-style banter blended with high-drama fear will glue our hineys to the couch most of the day. It is difficult for our children to become the leaders, innovators, creative souls they were meant to be with that echoing in their ears all day long.

As parents we need to model a life with little gossip.

I recall having a political conversation with friends in front of my twelve-year-old daughter. She left the room crying. When I asked her about it later she said we were gossiping. I had purposefully not gossiped about friends and colleagues in front of my kid. Somehow I thought political banter was different, not really gossip since it was about people who put themselves in the public eye. I realized that even talk about politicians and super-stars falls into the definition of gossip where secrets are told, our very complicated lives are judged and criticized, our weaknesses exaggerated, and our strengths are used against us.

One might wonder what this has to do with our teen's sexuality, or GPS systems or horses thirsty for answers about romance. The most common topics in gossip, the favorite themes in drama are sex and romance. I talk with teens daily who spread horrid gossip about what other teens are said to have done sexually. These same gossip-spreading teens have had the exact gossip spread about themselves. I sit with them as they sob and recount when someone called them gay or exaggerated an innocent flirt or told of an embarrassing sexual mistake. Yet days later they are doing the very same thing to another teen.

It is oddly fun and addictive to cast the first stone. Like eating Cheese Puffs, it isn't good for us and stains our fingers orange, but it's hard to stop once it's begun. Gossip really isn't good for teens because it distracts them from their education and creates hostile school communities, and because it ruins reputations and takes all the fun out of budding romance and sexuality.

Chapter 13:
Five Extra Minutes...

How was your day?

Would you empty the dishwasher?

Did you get that assignment handed in?

We want to go visit the Leadbetters this weekend. I know you don't, but you can't stay here alone. No, you can't. It'll be fun. We can go hiking. Amy will be there. You can hang out with your friends anytime.

You need what? How much is that? What did you do with that twenty I gave you?

Did you empty the dishwasher?

I have no idea how to do that math, you know that. Why didn't you go to the Math Lab after school?

Yes, you have to go this weekend. I am pretty sure that movie will be here next weekend.

No you and Amy can't drive if we go. I don't care if they are dirt roads. I do know you both have your permits, but it is still illegal.

No, you can't wear that tomorrow. Because I can see your bra straps. I don't care if no one cares about bra straps anymore. I do.

Did you empty the dishwasher?

I had to feed Fred this morning after you left. No, he did not have any food. Neither did Ella. I assume you haven't scooped the back yard either.

Really? That's a lot of ice cream.

How'd the test go? I know he hasn't graded them yet. How do you think it went? I told you to use flash cards, they might have helped.

Have you been working on that ACT book? Why not?

Excuse me, do not text while I am talking to you.

Wow, that looks great.

Did you empty the dishwasher?

We don't actually spend a lot of time talking to our teens every day, and most of the interactions seem critical or demanding. How about just adding five minutes a day? We spend way more than five minutes a day standing in line for our lattes, playing Angry Birds or Spider Solitaire, and checking our online social and interest accounts. Five extra minutes might give us the opportunity to add something like this:

I saw Mrs. Graham today at the store. She asked about you. She said you were always one of her favorites.

What do you want for dinner tomorrow night?

Thanks for cleaning up the TV room.

What are you reading these days? I just finished this book, you might like it.

I heard the new vampire movie is good.

Want to get some driving in tonight?

What's Bridget up to these days? We should have her over.

I want to show you this hilarious YouTube that your Aunt Vickie sent me.

Are things going any better in math?

Anything funny happen today?

Did you empty the dishwasher?

Chapter 14:
Men, Step Up

Men, it is your time. You are needed. Step-up Baby, because only you can help teen boys get back on track. Only you.

Historically, you've left this topic to wives and schools and churches. With the amount of cyber-influence and the sexual distortion that comes with it wives and schools and churches just don't have enough influence or information to help lead your sons into healthy sexual futures.

When I counsel dads about talking to their sons about sex they squirm. They say they remember being a teen. They feel like they don't have much right to talk to boys about things they feel they did poorly. It's like they don't want to say, "Avoid fast food" with Big Mac breath.

I tell them they don't have to tell their sons all about their sexual lives. I tell them they do need to tell them whatever they are comfortable with and to give them the basics; to talk. I tell them it will help lead these legions of porn zombies into the light where sexuality can be healthy and good, where it can lead to great connection and ultimately, happiness.

Boys need to know that you know they have access to and are probably watching porn. They need less judgment, guilt and condemnation to hell or to the therapist's office. They need to know it is a very strong temptation. They need to know that the stuff occurring in porn is fantasy and will not lead to good sex or relationships or lives. They need to know about slowing down. They need to know how both the male and female bodies work. They need to be told to stop asking girls for pictures and videos and sexually explicit chatting because of the legal exposure and reputation-wrecking consequences. They may need to know about self-pleasure. They need to know all the ways young women say "No." They need to know so very much and they need it from you.

Women just cannot do this the way men can.

In the TED Talk: The Demise of Guys, Philip Zimbardo speaks of the problems for boys and young men that have arisen from being constantly plugged-in to the cyber world. He notes apathy, school failure, under-functioning, and a lack of relationship and intimacy skills. The Demise of Guys can be stopped when men realize their importance. They will need to realize their powerful wisdom within their own confusion around sexuality.

Just as men must give half the ingredients to create a child, just as their hand strength must open the stuck jar, their knowledge of male sexuality, from wise to confusing, must educate our young men. Men, you could alter the course of history.

Chapter 15:
Abs Tin Ants Own Lee

Abstinence is a great word that helps kids wait to have sex. It is a word that kids can say clearly in this time when the cyber-world confuses them into stuttering. Phrases like "I'm waiting" give them a blissful boundary between their bodies and the other bodies whirling frantically around like bumper cars.

Adding *Only* to the end of Abstinence means waiting until marriage is the only correct way to become sexual. That is a hard pill to swallow, since ninety-five percent of us did not wait; since ninety-five percent of them will not wait.

Being part of that ninety-five percent, most parents know this, yet they keep adding *only* to the end of that helpful word. I ask parents time and time again what they hope for their kids' sexuality. They say, "I want them to wait until marriage." As a therapist I need to figure out if they mean it because seventy percent do not and thirty do. So I say, "Picture your kid's wedding." They look off into space and smile as they see their beautiful daughter/handsome son, out of college, grad school even, financially stable, lovely partner at their side, toasting the greatness of their parents. I jar them out of this future bliss. "How old are they?" They notice. He's 28, she's 26; the national age averages for marriage.

I don't even ask the question, "So, you think your sixteen-year-old son or daughter, revving like NASCAR before the checkered flag, is going to wait ten to twelve years before they push the pedal to the metal?"

I don't need to. Thirty percent of parents nod *yes*. Seventy percent smile like someone who has been caught in a lie.

About seventy percent of parents have no belief that their children will wait until marriage to become sexual. They admit that they hope if they tell their teens to wait until marriage they will wait until they are older. They really hope their kids wait until they move out of the house, go to college, or get an apartment. But they tell their kids *only*.

There are consequences to saying *only* to your kid when you don't believe it. Pre-adolescent kids love Abstinence Only. They love telling their parents they will wait until marriage. The thought of sex is disgusting to them anyway. Their parents give them purity rings and huge smiles. Then one day their bodies wake up sexually like all of ours did in our teens. They feel betrayed by their bodies and themselves. They feel guilty. But that sexual desire is not going away, and they begin to realize they probably will not be waiting until their dream wedding, late in their twenties. Feeling betrayed by one's body; feeling guilty for the God-given desires of budding sexuality; feeling like they will never be able to live out their promises to their parents is not the best way to a start a healthy sexual life.

Once they wake up sexually, these kids often believe it is all over. They think it is all or nothing, because that's what they were told. They think they should just go ahead and become sexual. They don't think about all the fun stuff along the way. They don't think about starting out as kissers. They don't think about going slow.

Every once in a while I get the privilege of talking to these kids before they go ahead and get 'er done. I give them permission to continue waiting and to get to know about their bodies and sexuality even though they are fairly sure they will not be waiting until their wedding day. They are always grateful. They often wait a very long time before becoming sexual.

The other thirty percent of parents honestly believe their children should and will wait until marriage. I absolutely honor their deep beliefs and try to help them find ways to assist their kids to this goal. I think it should be done without deceit, without denial, without high conflict and control. It is a tricky and mostly unsuccessful endeavor.

I am not the only one less-than-successful at insuring kids wait until marriage. Abstinence Only sex education programs have been in our public school systems for more a decade. Their success is highly debated, and statistics on higher percentages of teens getting pregnant or contracting an STI vary greatly. It seems about two percent more teens wait a few years past high school to become sexually active than before Abstinence Only education. The important statistic that has not changed is the percentage of people who wait until marriage to become sexual; that's still five percent and falling.

So education programs have not really worked. What might? There seem to be two camps of thought on sex education. One focuses on spiritual and moral beliefs, the other on practical safety and biological information.

When I talk to teens who are considering becoming sexual, I always ask them about their spiritual beliefs. Most of them say they believe God wants them to wait until marriage. I ask them if they are planning on waiting until marriage. Most of them say "No". I ask them how their relationship with God will be affected. They say things like, "Jesus will forgive me. He forgave my parents for divorcing. He forgave my dad for having an affair. He forgave my sister for getting pregnant." They have a great deal of faith in Jesus's ability to forgive.

When I talk to them about the possibility of getting pregnant or catching some STI, they say with the confidence of a super hero that they are invincible; that they know everything about sex and can take care of things. Though education, scare tactics and statistics do aid in postponement and safety they do not altered the premarital sex numbers.

A very few religions do well at ensuring that their kids wait until marriage to have sex. There are community consequences for having premarital sex, such as excommunication. Some religious communities do not allow those who have had sex outside of marriage to be married in the church without a long renewal-of-faith ritual. This is a huge cultural consequence that does help keep many young adults chaste. They also encourage young marriage. They encourage short engagements. These tactics seem to help young people follow their spiritual belief that sex should only occur after one is married. Fear of God does not seem to work. Fear of pregnancy does not seem to work. Anger from families does not seem to work. Huge social consequences and young marriage seem to work.

Yet many parents do not want their children to marry young. What does one do with that sexuality? Are they allowed or encouraged or discouraged to self-pleasure? Should they deny their sexual drives? How does one do that?

Creating sexually healthy individuals and requiring them to put their sexuality on ice for over a decade is a difficult task that has proved disastrous when it fails. The headlines report these failures of clergy, politicians and groups of believers who are required to do so. Their sexuality can turn aberrant; children are molested, porn becomes addictive, drugs and alcohol dull desires, secret lives are created.

So, what do you do? What do they do?

These are huge questions that have been explored for years with few, if any, solutions. The chance seems slim that the answers will come in time for our current youth to adopt.

Chapter 16:
Too Late

There comes a time when a kid is going to do it. There comes a time when the kid has done it. There comes a time when the decision has been made and the steep snowy hill rumbles and the avalanche occurs.

I know it the moment they walk through my door. I know that no matter what I say they will be having sex very soon; I know they have already had sex. The Ferrari will be driven. Nothing, no parental controls, no monitoring, no wise lectures, no guilt, no bribery, no duct tape is going to stop this from happening. Whether they already had sex or sex is imminent, the feel is exactly the same.

There are far more moments when they swagger in and say they are planning to have sex soon, but I know they are really begging me to keep them from having sex.

That's easy.

I tell them that just because they started to wake up sexually doesn't mean it is time for sex. I talk to them about the consequences of early and bad sexuality. *Why do it?*

I tell them how important it is to keep in relationship with their parents and their belief systems. I tell them to talk to their parents about it.

I ask them what they hope and dream for their entire sexual lives.

I point out how they must navigate their sexuality well to have healthy, connected and great sexual futures. I tell them about how negatively the cyber-world has influenced teen sexuality and how they must know about the consequences way before they begin exploring their sexuality.

That's the fun part of my job; giving kids permission to mindfully wait.

But then again, there are the moments when the waiting is over.

Parents suspect when their child is close to or beyond this point of no return. They come into my office furious or terrified or both. They desperately ask for advice on how to stop the avalanche. If the kid is simply testing the waters, and is double-daring the adults to give them wisdom then I have the best of advice for those parents.

The parents of kids who already have turned the key on that Ferrari's ignition or have already taken it around the block get different wisdom. This wisdom is a little more difficult because most parents wish that their children wouldn't have sex until they were physically and emotionally mature. To the parents who really hope their kid will wait until they marry this point of no return seems like the end of their highest hopes for their child.

Some of these revving kids choose poorly. They follow the model of porn to get 'er done and hook up with a less-than-worthy partner in a less-than-ideal setting with less-than-safe practices.

Some manage to do okay.

There are also the kids who are in committed, long-term relationships in high school. There aren't many who remain together for months and months and years, but the ones who do seem to navigate sex rather well, though sooner than most parents would prefer. They tend to slowly get to know one another sexually. They tend to be responsible and respectful. They tend to be safe. They tend to be less influenced by cyber-sexuality. They tend to have rather positive experiences.

Parents of these kids are frequently frustrated, because they often like their child's partner, but hate that the natural consequence of being romantic with another for a long period of time will most likely lead to sex. Parents try to control the time the kids have together. They try to break the couple up. They try to get them to marry young. They have some success. They have a good deal of failure. It's always a quandary, because these young lovers frequently come from happily married families, and are simply reenacting healthy relationships. They just started young.

So what do you do when they already have?

Sixty percent of kids have had sex by their high school graduation day. Within the year following high school that number rises to eighty percent. These statistics have not changed significantly in decades. Whether this indicates a moral and spiritual crisis or unhealthy communities or simply truths about our sexual bodies and desires and instincts does not matter. Parents might claim that this should not be, but our kids are living these statistics that obviously will take a great deal to alter.

If your kid is riding that avalanche, if it is too late to stop them from having sex, what do you do?

It is easy to get stuck in wondering how this occurred. You could blame yourself for not giving her good wisdom or for having a cold home or for not monitoring his behavior enough. You could blame others for not parenting well or the Internet for stimulating them into early sex. It doesn't matter because we cannot know all the reasons and causes. More than likely our teen's choice to become sexual has to do with a perfect storm of reasons including our parenting and hormones and opportunities over which we have no control. The attention of a beautiful Venus or a big smiling demi-god can start the most stable of mountain slopes rumbling.

Again, what do you do? Many parents I work with seem to give up, believing their influence on their kid is over once they become sexual. The chill in their home becomes a blizzard. Their monitoring becomes non-existent or brutally controlling. The kid stands alone right when they need wisdom more than ever. The high-risk consequences of early sex become imminent: pregnancy, many partners, no birth control, drug and alcohol abuse, domestic abuse, STI, depression, and high drama relationships.

What do you do? If your kid took the family car for a ride around the block before he got his license, would you throw up your hands, hand him the keys and quit talking to him? Or would you continue giving driving lessons, monitor his behavior closer and give him more wisdom about driving? If they got into a wreck would you withhold medical treatment?

Kids who have sex, especially in these days of cyber-influenced sex, are often confused and disappointed and injured. Without compassion and wisdom they tend to simply continue on.

There are programs that encourage sexually active kids become virginal again. I have not found those to be very helpful, because they do not acknowledge the kid's reality. It's like trying to make a toddler crawl again. Once they toddle, we simply have to help them navigate their environment. That being said, you can encourage kids to slow down. You can let them know that just because they had sex they don't have to keep having sex. You can encourage them to get to know their bodies better, to know more about sex and the cyber influences. You can certainly continue to encourage them to wait.

If your kid has crossed the line, if your kid has become sexual don't abandon him or her. Continue on with your wisdom, warmth and monitoring; maybe even more so.

Chapter 17:
Quality

During presentations on wise parenting, I ask parents to create a bumper sticker, not one their teens will really put on their cars, but a concise sentence that reflects what they would love to say to their teens about sex. They write things like: *Wait until marriage. Be safe. Be healthy. Be in love. Be over eighteen.* When I began writing my book on sex for my daughter, I decided to create my own bumper sticker. I thought I would write *Wait until you move out of my house.* I figured by then she'd be old enough to make more mature choices, and God knows I have heard hundreds of horror stories about parents walking in on their teens having sex. Yet as I pondered what I really hoped for her, these surprising words formed: *I hope your first experience is really nice. I hope you have a great sex life.*

What? Why would I even think such a thing? Really nice? Where did that come from?

I mean I was certainly part of the seventy percent who had little belief that my kid would wait until she was married to have sex. I hadn't waited even though I had pledged Abstinence at my church. Still, I had waited a very long time, like an after-college long time.

Before I wrote her the book I had not mentioned that. I didn't say anything. I let her listen to the Abstinence Only education given at her school and never said, "...well yes, that is a fine option, but you may be one of the 95% of us who didn't wait." I let her believe all adults had waited the way I let her believe in the Easter Bunny and the Tooth Fairy. Thinking at some point she'd figure it out, like the night I awoke to find my dad shoving a quarter under my pillow, my old tooth in hand.

While researching the book I started answering the questions in Chapter Five about how I became sexual and I remembered. I remembered what helped and what didn't.

I recalled when my body woke up. I'd been a huge proponent of Abstinence Only. My church, my parents' silence, my beliefs, and horror stories all kept my preadolescent body sure of its righteous stand that I would never have sex, much less have sex before I was married.

And then it happened. Huge. Everything. My straight, flat body curved and blossomed. My sweet, pure mind began to pole dance with sexual thoughts and desires. I recall exactly when my body woke up.

I remember my church discouraged us from dancing and dating and holding hands and kissing. I recall after youth groups we would all go out and dance and date and hold hands and kiss...a lot. The pastor's sermons did not stop my body from revving. It did not stop me from wanting answers. It didn't stop me from envisioning doing all sorts of things with this body.

There was no one to talk to because my parents denied the existence of this inner-Ferrari. My sister and brother were years ahead of me on this journey so they would have teased and taunted and exposed my fragile wings to their sexually seasoned friends. My own friends' engines had not yet turned over and they would proclaim me a sexual mutant. I was on my own.

I prayed. Really, I did. I asked God for the driver's manual.

God answered.

Within one week I had two books in my hand. For me they were the equivalent of the Old and New Testament to my Sexual Bible.

The first came to me at a yard sale. For a quarter I got a perfect copy of *Our Bodies, Ourselves*. It told me everything I needed to know about how the body functions sexually, how menstrual cycles and pregnancy and health and infections work. It told me about arousal and masturbation and all the steps from attraction to intercourse. It told me these things straight-faced and without judgment.

It also had an index that was as magic as any book found at Hogwarts. There was nothing you could ask of this index that it could not reference: orgasm, discharge, lubrication, wet dreams, and the recipe for hollandaise sauce. I swear it never let me down. As any and all questions were answered, this nasty, foreign body transformed into a miraculous gift.

The other book God gave me, the New Testament, appeared in the bookshelf of a wonderful woman I cleaned house for. She was wealthy and fun and successful. She was one of the happiest women I have ever met. She worked on Saturdays so I had the entire day to come in and clean. It took two hours. I often went early, cleaned and then enjoyed hanging out in her beautiful and quiet home. I turned on the high-end stereo, painted my nails with expensive nail polish and read her grown-up books and magazines. The week I asked God for the driver's manual I found a book I'd never seen on her shelves before, a huge book with the words *The Joy of Sex* across its binding.

The Joy of Sex. Its lettering looked so similar to my mother's copy of *The Joy of Cooking* I thought it was series of books on pleasurable things. I still search bookstores for the latest volume, like *The Joy of Dancing, The Joy of Laughter* or *The Joy of Sleeping-In*.

What I recall about that book was page after page of pencil drawings of a naked couple in hundreds of sexual positions. I was horrified and enthralled. I could not put that book down. It was my very first visual instruction on sexuality. It was my instant model. Its images are burned in my mind. The images told me sex is creative, calm, passionate, kind, playful, respectful, loving and joyful.

What do the pornographic images our children see first teach them about sex?

The knowledge given me by these books did not encourage me to drive recklessly into sex. I valued my body and my sexuality so much that every time I was in a position to intersect with another revving teen I assessed his sexual ability. I assessed the physical, emotional and spiritual quality of the possible encounter. I said "No" without fear or guilt or pressure. I said "No" with the calm power of one who deeply knows her worth.

What if, along with belief systems and biological sex education, we add the issue of quality? There is a lot of fear around teaching kids about sex and sexuality. There fear is that it will give them an open door into early sex. It could. I am sure it can, but I have found that along with moral teachings, along with information about the possible negative consequences of sex, when we also address the issue of quality sexual lives versus mindless sexual lives they wait far longer and make far better choices. It respects the fact that their bodies have been switched on sexually by God himself. It gives them a different model than the always-ready-to-instruct pornography that fills our airwaves and their minds.

PART IV:
YOU'VE ARRIVED AT YOUR DESTINATION

I need to remind myself.

Every single time a kid has spoken to me about these things with eyes ready to harden I give them wisdom, I give them directions, I tell them the truth. Every single time their heads nod as they take mental notes. A wave of relief washes over them. They do that unusual thing my kid did when I gave her the book I wrote on sex, they thank me. They hold my gaze. The next time I see them they no longer feel like victims, but like powerful, confident and, dare I say, happy teens, because romance and sex just became less terrifying. Now they have ways to protect themselves. Now they understand what has been so distorted. Now they realize they are not alone in this confusion. Now they see a possibility for the tender connection they have been dreaming of all their lives. They are quick studies.

I need to remind myself this happens every single time I have the opportunity to share this wisdom. A twenty minute conversation and they have it. They really want the truth. The solution to this unexpected consequence of handing our kids cell phones, computers, gaming systems and music pods can be mitigated by as little as one conversation.

I need to remind myself this plugged-in crew is oddly prepared to take in information, alter their own behaviors and encourage their peers to do the same. They do so with intensity. They do so quickly. They do so with amazing social skills.

81

Chapter 18:
Dude...Good News

Even though they have been swimming in cyber-sexuality and entertainment inspired gossip and drama, today's teens are totally cool, way cooler than we are. They're funnier, too. They have great hair products. They love sushi and lattes. They sing and dance. They gather and send cyber-items of interest to everyone. They talk to adults as equals. They stand up to bullies. They crack me up.

Plus, they have the word *Dude*. We don't. Not really. We're probably too late for *Dude*.

Dude.

I really can't say enough about the power of this word and the teens that use it, because *Dude* acknowledges connection and worth, and disarms conflicts all in four letters, one syllable.

After nearly twenty-five years of studying teen linguistics and happening upon the wonder of the word *Dude*, I may just be the only Dude-ologist out there. I have made some observations and come to some conclusions.

Dude is used in two ways. The first instantly acknowledges one's status as an equal, a friend, a brother or sister, one who belongs right where they are. *Dude*! It means welcome, I missed you, you belong here, it is good to see you, now we are all here.

Dude also, brilliantly, takes all conflict down a few notches, conflicts that make adults instantly raise hackles, draw lines, shut out information, judge, criticize, devalue, discount and divide. *Dude* douses a raging inferno into a small flame that can be used as a light as well as a marshmallow toaster, and not as a flame thrower or bomb igniter.

It brings the volume level of anger, fear, and distrust down from of Battle to Conversation. It changes the goal from dominance to expanded visions.

It is flipping brilliant.

Dude!

Angry drunks, scorned hearts, embarrassed souls, and open wounds, are all soothed with the word that says, "Chill out. It isn't worth it. You belong. You are of worth. You are my brother. I've been there, we all have. Exhale. Enjoy this moment with me."

It is the ultimate tool for negotiation and these Dudes have it and use it like the best trained ambassadors for good will.

I bow to them, because though we adults may use it...we don't mean it. We don't really know the equal worth of all our fellow human beings and we don't really desire to douse the first flames of conflict. Not usually. Not really. These young souls are different.

So though they dog-paddle through adolescence often neck deep in porn and drama and gossip, they do have this secret weapon. It does keep them afloat and keeps them basically on course.

Chapter 19:
The Rest of the Good News

Today's plugged-in teens are as deep and shallow, wise and ignorant, kind and cruel as the rest of us. Yet because of the intimate relationship they have had with technology since early childhood their very psychology is different than that of we who acquired this technology later in life. New books on child development need to be written. We've talked about the negative effects their cyber-connected life has had on their sexual development. It is time to celebrate the positive consequences it has had on their lives.

Since the industrial revolution, when folks moved from extended family and community to tiny nuclear units in privacy-obsessed cities, most of us have swam in the angsty waters of isolation. The most common complaint that brings folks into therapy is their feeling of unhappiness, and their main issue tends to be feeling isolated. There is a deep cultural insecurity about where one fits in and what worth they have. It used to be when I spoke to teens I could make an instant bond with them around the "fact" that we all feel lonely and disconnected. Our eyes would meet in painful understanding, but no longer.

Talk to teens about feeling lonely. Because it is a cultural norm to discuss weather and sports and how no one likes us too very much, they may give a perfunctory they never write, they never call sort of response. But listen beyond their words and look into their screen-reflecting eyes. When you talk about true loneliness they really are bewildered. For they are texted, poked, twittered and *wassuped* so many times a day they need never feel lonely. Each ding of a phone or laptop conveys a tiny message of "Hey, I'm thinking about you." Hundreds of times a day they are told with a playful cyber-shove of their shoulder, "you belong."

Mom! Dad!

It used to be that those who did not fit into the main-stream ideals of looks and popularity and success were in acned-isolation, but now anyone can find kindred cyber-friends (or more likely swarms of them). Whether they connect because they love a game, movie or rock band, or they identify as a nerd or poet or with a belief system, there is a place for them real enough to be full of real people with whom they belong.

Yes, as in flesh life, negative interactions do occur like exploiting and bullying, but it is far easier to block negatives in the cyber world, and even the bullied find solace with other bullied kids. There are extreme examples, but there are far more kids feeling secure in their place in the cyber world and in their innate right to belong than in many generations before them. Most of the extreme negative examples are due to cyber-sexual and high gossip/drama issues.

We became adults in a time when only the wealthy, the social elite, the highly educated and the incredibly talented had voice; only their words were heard, were published, were of worth. Our kids publish every thought, every attempt, every hilarious moment of their lives. And they get instant feedback from *Like It* to *Really Dude?* The playing field is now incredibly equal. Everyone can now influence others. All ideas can be shared. Everyone can be a star. Everyone can influence public policy, because with a click of a key opinions are tallied everywhere from The Voice studios to Capitol Hill.

We all influence the world now, and our kids know it.

Mom! Dad!

Because they have been plugged in since they were quite young, their childhood curiosity has been tended to well and it flourishes. They look up every question. No one tells them to be quiet. No one judges their curiosity. They ask and search and, more important, they integrate all this information they gather and think bigger and wider than we who birthed them.

Adults were taught that a little self-importance is as bad as a little knowledge. Forget that. We may be handing them inheritances of huge economic, social, technological and environmental challenges, but dang, they really do have far better abilities to problem solve and collaborate than we do.

Mom! Dad!

The Internet entered our lives after our identities were formed, after our emotional and cognitive strategies went from pliable to mostly rigid. Our children's psychology formed with these cyber-gifts of understanding our intimate connection to all, our equal and innate worth, and instant access to most of the knowledge and wisdom ever created.

There is a huge fork in our kids' road. One takes all this greatness and distorts it with false, twisted and unhealthy sexuality; a sexuality that exploits, injures, embarrasses and disappoints into apathy. The other adds to their cyber-infused world a healthy sexuality; a sexuality that connects with intimacy, compassion and leads to—hallelujah--happiness.

Remember happiness? It's North, where we are connected intimately to others and community, where we can problem solve and be creative, where we are content.

You have arrived at your destination.

Chapter 20:
If Not The Wise We...

If not the wise We
Then who? Them,
Who also do not have the wise We?
Let us, along with the platter
Of spoiled meats and molded
Cheeses gift ripe
Figs and fresh oysters
So they can know the difference and choose.
They will choose.

These twenty-minus,
Those who know not loneliness
Never have,
Plugged in, twittered, texted, poked into
Knowing what we carefully forgot,
That we are all connected;
Every day, every moment, every thought,
Every beat of every heart,
Every tear, smile, inspiration,
Act of kindness, cruelty,
Greed, generosity.
They know.

They speak unfettered by
Degree or college or status
Or perfection, they speak
Though we were silenced by all
The above.
They blog and post and
Proclaim mundane and
Profane and profound alike.
They speak and know
Their worth.
They know. They search with googled curiosity.
They ask and receive currency in
Knowledge. They knit
And weave and make
Tapestries from scraps.
They know, those
Under twenties.
This is good because we hand
Them platters of confusion; rancid-bitter and
Cotton-candy sweet ingredients for their
Futures:
Political, global, environmental, economic,
Goo.
What champions they must be,
The platters have been filled, all
We can gift them now is our wisdom,
Cool water on scorching days,
Smooth calm voiced directions
Through and out.
That is enough.

References

"1 in 3 Boys Heavy Porn Users, Study Shows,"
ScienceBlog.com, http://scienceblog.com/12663/1-in-3-boys-heavy-porn-users-study-shows/

Albert, Bill. "With Once Voice 2007: America's Adults and Teens Sound Off About Teen Pregnancy," *The National Campaign to Prevent Teen Pregnancy*, February 2007, 7–8. http://www.thenationalcampaign.org/resources/pdf/pubs/WO V2007_fulltext.pdf (September 1, 2008).

Armstrong, Elizabeth A., England, Paula and Alison C. K. Fogarty. "Accounting for Women's Orgasm and Sexual Enjoyment in College Hookups and Relationships." *American Sociological Review* DOI: 10.1177/0003122412445802. Published online 7 May 2012.

Baron, Robert A., Byrne, Donna, and Branscombe, Nyla R. *Social Psychology, Eleventh Edition.* Allyn and Bacon. 2007.

Brown, Jon. "Sexual Abuse: A Public Health Challenge." *NSPCC.* October 2011

Cacilda, Jetha and Ryan, Christopher. *Sex at Dawn.* Harper Perennial. 2010.

Cottle, Thomas J. "Getting beyond Self-Esteem." *Childhood Education 80* (Mid-Summer 2004): 269–271.

De Angelis, Tori. "Web Pornography Effect on Children." *Monitor on Psychology.* Vol. 30, #10, November 2007.

Dines, Gail. *Pornland.* Beacon Press. Boston, Massachusetts, 2010.

Doheny, Kathleen. "Ten Surprising Health Benefits of Sex." *WebMD.com.* May 27, 2012. http://www.webmd.com/sex-relationships/features/10-surprising-health-benefits-of-sex

Finer, Lawrence. "Trends in Premarital Sex in the United States, 1954 – 2003". *Public Health Reports.* January/February 2007.

Guilamo-Ramos V., Jaccard J, and Dittus, P. *Parental Monitoring of Adolescents: Current Perspectives for Researchers and Practitioners.* New York: Columbia University Press. 2010.

"Households and Families." Living Cities: The National Community Development Initiative. *Seattle in Focus: A Profile from Census 2000.*

Lenhart, Amanda. "Pew Internet & American Life Project. How Do They Even Do That?" A Pew Internet Guide to Teens, Mobile phones and Social Media. *M Communications Studies.* June 2010.

Lieberman, Lisa. "Early Predictors of Sexual Behavior: Implications for Young Adolescents and Their Parents." *Perspectives on Sexual and Reproductive Health,* Volume 38, Number 2, June 2006.

Markham C.M., Lormand D., and Gloppen K.M. "Connectedness as a Predictor of Sexual and Reproductive Health Outcomes for Youth." *Journal of Adolescent Health* 2010;46(3 Suppl 1):S23–S41.

Martino, Steven C., Elliott, Marc N., Corona, Rosalie and others. "Beyond the "Big Talk": The Roles of Breadth and Repetition in Parent-Adolescent Communication About Sexual Topics."

Pediatrics. March 2008; 121:2 e612-e618;doi:10.1542/peds. 2007-2156

McNeely,C.A., Shew, M.L., Beuhring, T., et al. "Mothers' Influence on Adolescents' Sexual Debut." *Journal of Adolescent Health*, 31(3), 2002.

"Median Age At First Marriage for Women." U.S. Census Bureau. (May 21, 2011)

"Median Age At First Marriage for Men. U.S. Census Bureau. (May 21, 2011)

Meschke, Laurie, Bartholomae, Suzanne, and Zentall, Shannon R. "Adolescent Sexuality and Parent-Adolescent Processes: Promoting Healthy Teen Choices. *Journal of Adolescent Health.* Volume 31,Issue 6, Supplement. December 2002. 264-279.

"Parent Guide to Internet Safety." FBI Reports and Publications.

"Parents, Peers, Pressure: Identifying the Influences on Responsible Sexual Decision-Making." *National Association of Social Workers.* Vol. 2, No. 2, September 2001.

Regnerus, Mark. *Forbidden Fruit.* Oxford University Press, 2007.

Regnerus, Mark and Uecker, Jeremy. *Premarital Sex in America.* Oxford University Press, 2011.

Rideout, Victoria J., Vandewater, Elizabeth A., and Wartella, Ellen A. " Zero to Six: Electronic Media Influence in the lives of Infants, Toddlers and Preschoolers." *A Kaiser Foundation Family Report.* Fall 2003.AA

Sieving, R.E., McNeely, C.A. and Blum, R.W. "Maternal Expectations, Mother-Child Connectedness, and Adolescent Sexual Debut." *Archives of Pediatric Adolescent Medicine,* 154(8):809-816, 2000.

"Sexting: Youth Practices and Legal Implications." The Berkman Center for Internet & Society at Harvard University. Georgia Code. ADL.

Schurgin, Gwenn and Clarke-Pearson, Kathleen. COUNCIL ON COMMUNICATIONS AND MEDIA. March 2011

Wilcox, W. Bradford. "The State of Our Unions: When Marriage Disappears." *National Marriage Project.* University of West Virginia. 2011.

Windle, Michael, Brener, Nancy, Cuccaro, Paul, and others. "Parenting Predictors of Early-Adolescent Health Behaviors". Journal of Youth and Adolescence, *v 39, no. 6, June 2010, 594 –606.*

Veenhoven, R. "Bibliography of Happiness." *World Database of Happiness.* Erasmus University Rotterdam. Assessed 2012-5-1 at http://worlddatabase.eur.nl

Zambardo, Philip. "Demise of Guys." *TED Talk.* Oct 2010.

About the Author

Elizabeth Clark has been counseling teens for twenty-five years. She's spent the past ten years trying to unravel why teen sexuality has been so negatively impacted by their constant access to plugged-in technology. She has come to some simple and successful solutions on how to help them navigate through the cyber-sexual landscape they have access to twenty-four hours a day.

Elizabeth lives in the high desert of Colorado where she hikes and bikes on red sandstone, plays with words and dogs, and admires the dazzle in the souls who choose to sit on her couch.

CPSIA information can be obtained at www.ICGtesting.com
Printed in the USA
BVOW081618141012

302805BV00001BA/4/P